T0294512

Museum Finance

American Alliance of Museums

The American Alliance of Museums has been bringing museums together since 1906, helping to develop standards and best practices, gathering and sharing knowledge, and providing advocacy on issues of concern to the entire museum community. Representing more than 35,000 individual museum professionals and volunteers, institutions, and corporate partners serving the museum field, the Alliance stands for the broad scope of the museum community.

The American Alliance of Museums' mission is to champion museums and nurture excellence in partnership with its members and allies.

Books published by AAM further the Alliance's mission to make standards and best practices for the broad museum community widely available.

 American Alliance of Museums

Museum Finance

Issues, Challenges, and Successes

Brian Alexander

ROWMAN & LITTLEFIELD
Lanham • Boulder • New York • London

Published by Rowman & Littlefield
An imprint of The Rowman & Littlefield Publishing Group, Inc.
4501 Forbes Boulevard, Suite 200, Lanham, Maryland 20706
www.rowman.com

86-90 Paul Street, London EC2A 4NE

British Library Cataloguing in Publication Information Available

Library of Congress Cataloging-in-Publication Data

Names: Alexander, Brian, 1951- author.
Title: Museum finance : issues, challenges, and successes / Brian
   Alexander.
Description: Lanham : Rowman & Littlefield, [2023] | Publication supported
   by the American Alliance of Museums. | Includes bibliographical
   references and index. | Summary: "Here is a comprehensive guide to
   financial management and stability for museums that provides context for
   the financial issues faced by museums and offer suggestions to mitigate
   them. It will help the reader understand why finances are chronic
   issues, provide perspective to see challenges more clearly, and offer
   advice to fix them"-- Provided by publisher.
Identifiers: LCCN 2022045823 (print) | LCCN 2022045824 (ebook) |
   ISBN 9781538138328 (cloth) | ISBN 9781538138335 (paperback)|
   ISBN 9781538138342 (ebook)
Subjects: LCSH: Museum finance--United States. | Museums--United
   States--Management.
Classification: LCC AM122 .A63 2023 (print) | LCC AM122 (ebook) |
   DDC 069/.0681--dc23/eng/20220922
LC record available at https://lccn.loc.gov/2022045823
LC ebook record available at https://lccn.loc.gov/2022045824

∞™ The paper used in this publication meets the minimum requirements of American National Standard for Information Sciences—Permanence of Paper for Printed Library Materials, ANSI/NISO Z39.48-1992.

For Audrey

Contents

Acknowledgments

The idea for this book began as a finance class assignment in which students at the Cooperstown Graduate Program in Museum Studies were asked to research and compile weekly museum finance-related news stories to share with classmates. The purpose of the assignment was to acquaint students with the types of financial experiences, both positive and negative, that they might encounter when they enter the museum field. The surprisingly large number of stories found by students made clear the potential usefulness of continued research to better understand a fuller range of typical financial challenges. It was hoped that this additional research would help museum leaders better anticipate and understand museum financial issues, challenges, and solutions.

Since the initial classroom investigation, graduate researchers continued their work thanks to a grant from the Faculty Research & Creative Activity Grant Program of the State University of New York, College at Oneonta. Research was accelerated, and what started as a modest class project with a small number of articles rapidly developed into a database of hundreds of news stories on museum finance. These articles became the basis for this book. Special thanks to student research assistant Karina Kowalski, who conducted extensive research and established and organized our database of news stories. Thanks also to the finance students at the Cooperstown Graduate Program, especially Alexis DiBartolomeo, Ashley Gallagher, Mary Zell Galen, and Tucker Broadbooks.

Lastly, thanks to editor Charles Harmon and his unflagging patience and support throughout the project.

Preface

Museum Finance: Issues, Challenges, and Successes is a book about museum financial triumphs and challenges as covered by the news media along with my own perspectives. It illustrates stories that were felt to be newsworthy and in the public interest. Whether negative or positive, the stories touch on the full universe of financial challenges faced by museums. The goal of the project was not to create a definitive study of each organization's issues and what went wrong or right, but to shine a light in general on certain patterns of financial management in museums.

The book looks at stories primarily from the last twenty years or so, and case studies are illustrated largely through news reports of the time. Hundreds of news articles were reviewed, and the stories illustrated varying levels of financial success or distress. It became clear that the scenarios of financial triumph, frustration, and failure were remarkably similar. The size, discipline, or location of the museum did not seem to matter, nor did the size of its budgets. It was the nature of the problems that fell into predictable patterns. Each story revealed an important, instructional window into the financial realities faced by today's museums. As a museum director and chief executive officer for nearly forty years, I found the stories familiar ones—the struggle to be financially sustainable, the search for new revenue streams, limited oversight and checks and balances, unfounded optimism over revenue projections, and lack of engagement in financial matters. These stories were balanced with ones of decisive museum leadership, trustee solidarity, institutional courage, creative entrepreneurship, and effective planning.

Many institutions recognized their financial struggles early and took aggressive action to address them. Instituting financial discipline, expanding fundraising activity, tightening budgets, diversifying revenue streams, being more entrepreneurial, growing organically, and planning effectively were among the initiatives that rescued many organizations and put them on a healthier financial track. Other organizations waited until they found themselves at a financial crossroads and had little choice but to respond in crisis mode.

Some institutions encountered difficulty when it became apparent that many issues were internally inflicted; that is, problems developed not because of uncontrollable circumstances (such as poor economy, weather, or the pandemic), but rather from inattention to financial matters. Often it seemed as though finances were not given priority until an existential crisis presented itself. This "late to the game" approach made recovery more difficult, but many still prevailed by instituting drastic and painful measures.

The book begins with a look at why museum finance is inherently challenging and how difficult it is to balance the need to generate adequate funding while providing accessible, meaningful mission-based services. Many institutions took action by being bold, innovative, and even controversial. Others had difficulty keeping up with the times, diversifying revenue sources, and practicing financial oversight.

Chapter 3, "Blending Money and Mission," discusses how financial conditions forced institutions to become more resourceful and entrepreneurial, often freeing up traditional ways of doing things in favor of activities that were both more relevant and cost-effective. Related to this was the search for revenue diversification and how relying too much on one or two sources of revenue can be problematic if those sources are diminished or disappear completely. Yet diversification must be approached carefully; the reasons for and goals of diversification must be clear, and both the pros and cons must be considered.

The next chapter explores expansion activity in museums and the lure of expansion. While done with the best of intentions, it is often unaffordable and results in serious crises because a situation may be created in which the museum cannot afford to complete the expansion or operate it effectively once the expansion is completed.

Chapter 6, "Taking Care of Business," makes the case that every organization, within reason, can control its finances, even with limited staff and other resources. This begins by deciding that finance is critically important and a key organizational responsibility. It must be given proper attention and consideration. This means that everyone has a role and every member of the museum family must have a good understanding of the museum's financial challenges. If everyone is paying attention, better decisions are made. This begins with the oversight level of trustees and extends throughout the entire organization.

The final chapter summarizes major points and focuses on the importance of careful planning prior to embarking on major initiatives; the value of learning from others' experiences; being realistic and not deferring difficult decisions; embracing entrepreneurship before reaching a state of desperation; diversifying revenue efforts carefully; paying attention to finances at all times; and ensuring that everyone has a role and all voices are heard.

The purpose of this study is to help museum leaders at all levels recognize and avoid certain financial minefields and realize that while there are financial hurdles in the museum world, they are solvable.

1

Understanding Museum Finance

Even though museums contribute significantly (nearly $50 billion) to the United States economy each year, the majority of the thirty-five thousand museums in the United States face some degree of financial challenges.[1] These challenges are the result of many factors, but the fundamental structural model of museum funding tops the list.

Museums, in pursuit of their public trust responsibilities to serve the common good, provide a wide range of services to the public. These include exhibitions, educational programs, public events, collections care, and preservation of historic structures, to name just a few. Activities such as these are at the very heart of a museum's reason for being, but they are costly, and the museum consumer alone cannot afford to underwrite their total costs. Doing so would make museum services prohibitively expensive for the consumer and significantly impact an institution's ability to make itself widely accessible.

Unlike for-profit businesses, museums do not rely solely on their core products or services to generate sustainable revenue streams to pay for the services they provide. Such a funding model seems untenable, and to an extent it is—what enterprise knowingly enters into a line of business in which its primary products are destined to run deficits?—yet this is true of most museums. As a result, museums find themselves focusing on two major, distinct lines of business that are conducted simultaneously. The first is mission fulfillment, or their *raison d'être*—they exist to serve the public and make their important work widely accessible. The second is revenue production, which provides the means by which museums accomplish their missions. Nothing happens without money. These two lines of business are inextricably linked, and balancing the effective pursuit of mission with the need to generate adequate and appropriate revenue streams is a tricky business.

Museums spend an inordinate amount of time and resources searching for predictable funding sources to sustain mission activities, yet they must do it in such a way that balances revenue production with mission-driven purposes. For example, increasing admission fees might seem a logical way to increase revenue, but doing so may result in lower visitation because it creates barriers for audiences who cannot afford higher fees. While keeping fees reasonable helps make programs more accessible to the public, it also puts more of a burden on the museum to find supplemental funding to make such programs possible. Ironically, the more museums focus on and expand mission-related activities, the more likely they find themselves facing financial challenges because of the increased pressures of sharing the true cost with the user.

Conversely, trimming program budgets may reduce expenditures, but this may also dilute quality programs and thus become less appealing to visitors. Such reductions may also create a scenario in which donors find a museum less appealing because it has reduced mission-based services and donors decide they will no longer support the museum. In other cases, programs may be crowd-pleasing and profitable but inconsistent with the mission, while other programs may be popular and meaningful, but not financially viable. Balancing mission *and* money often becomes a veritable magic trick and is challenging for even the most skilled museum administrators.

Charging fees equivalent to the actual cost of developing and presenting a program often cannot be fully absorbed by the museum's visitors, program participants, and other museum constituents. This is because the *full* cost of providing services is very likely to be prohibitively expensive to most consumers. And because museum-related services are not considered essential (at least to most people), patrons have a limit on what they are willing or able to pay for discretionary, leisure-time activities. Thus, museums deliberately depress fees to encourage maximum accessibility and are forced to search endlessly for creative ways to bridge the funding gap, such as fundraising and various earned income activities.

Some museums have been successful in creating this balance, while others have had more difficulty. What is clear, however, is this: The search for sustainable funding is an existential issue for museums and is being addressed through a wide range of responses. These vary from bold, aggressive mission and business initiatives to more modest, affordable approaches to minor, temporary fixes. Sometimes they are reliant on just plain, wishful thinking. Issues of funding are at the center of every museum conversation and drive virtually every institutional decision. Those who are unable to balance the programmatic and financial realities face a difficult road.

It has become essential for museums to employ entrepreneurial and business skills that often do not come naturally to many museum leaders. Entrepreneurial thinking and risk-taking may not be part of an institution's organizational culture; a director's career path may not have included business experience; there may be an unwillingness to try something new; the notion of change is just plain difficult; or change is seemingly an assault on the organization's long-held mission or values. But for those who are willing and able to change, and navigate it in a thorough and thoughtful manner, the outcome can be programmatically and financially dramatic.

Most museum administrators struggle with these fundamental tensions. The pressure is enormous and the variables unending. Keeping pace with technology in operations and exhibitions; serving the growing needs and expectations of an increasingly sophisticated audience; maintaining an aging museum infrastructure; attracting and supporting professional staff; living with decreased governmental funding; and navigating political pressures from donors or trustees are just a few of the financial stressors—and layered over each is the need to make the museum increasingly accessible and financially viable. Money has become the driving force of museum operations.

It is easy to see why many museums find themselves facing financial challenges. Many institutions find it difficult to think about long-term financial viability when they are consumed by the short-term financial pressures of meeting the next payroll, fixing the plumbing, or just keeping the doors open. Yet, if they don't think about and plan for the future and adapt to changing demands and expectations, their organizations will be left behind. Doing nothing is not an option, but doing too much too soon is risky and may jeopardize the museum's future. Risks are necessary to an institution's survival, of course, but sometimes risks are overly optimistic or even reckless and the organization finds itself in a worse state than ever.

Sometimes there is no choice but to take risks. When there is major infrastructure failure, it must be repaired or replaced. If there are no cash reserves, money must be borrowed or raised. Borrowing is a logical option, but borrowing must be repaid. Loan payments then add to monthly expenses, which is the last thing an institution in financial distress needs, as it makes an already-difficult cash-flow situation even worse. Sometimes money is borrowed from within an institution—usually the endowment—but there is little to enforce repayment and the loan has a way of not being repaid. And if it is not repaid, the endowment does not grow and actually produces *less* revenue than before the borrowing. The only way to navigate this positively is to raise money, which may or may not be within the institution's capabilities, and it can be a long process without any guarantees.

Complicating matters further is concern about attracting new visitors and making existing visitors want to return. These issues include such things as rising visitor sophistication and expectations; incorporating the latest technology into exhibitions; competing with other leisure-time activities;

demonstrating continued relevance; and keeping funders happy. The list goes on and on—and they all have financial implications.

Yet if these and other concerns are addressed too quickly, risks may be incurred that are beyond an institution's ability to effectively manage them. Museums must be simultaneously aggressive and patient while recognizing the limits of their tolerance for risk. Risks must be carefully calculated leaps of faith, but not reckless, death-defying leaps. Failure must not result in existential crises; instead, museums must proceed carefully in a measured, thoughtful, and organic fashion. Successful and healthy museums should accept risk as a central part of their business; minimize that risk by proceeding in a cautious and well-calculated manner; focus on those things that are within their reasonable control; and manage those things effectively.

This brings us to an important truth about many of the financial challenges faced by museums. While it is certainly true that many issues are externally imposed, they are only part of the problem. Many problems are simply the result of being too eager; lacking patience; feeling the pressure to move forward; or not giving financial matters the attention they deserve—in other words, these are self-imposed problems that can be remedied with more training, careful management, and thoughtful decision-making.

Many museums have fallen victim to confusion about authority; ill-considered or premature decision-making; overly optimistic revenue projections; risky expansion initiatives; or lack of careful planning. In other cases, museums have found themselves in financial distress because of a lack of regular financial oversight. Some issues have been relatively minor in nature and museums learned from their mistakes and eventually recovered. Others, however, were more existential in nature and had serious consequences for the long-term financial well-being of the institution. Naturally, some factors were simply beyond the control of museum leaders: COVID-19, poor weather, loss of government funding, a slowing economy, etc. Even so, it must be acknowledged that many issues could have been avoided if more attention had been paid to financial matters.

There are many examples of financial challenges faced by museums. The good news is that many of these issues can be significantly mitigated through more rigorous management and conscientious, regular oversight. Hopefully, an awareness of typical problems—how they happen and what organizations do to fix them—will help museums avoid similar difficulties.

NOTE

1. "New National Data Reveals the Economic Impact of Museums Is More Than Double Previous Estimates," *American Alliance of Museums*, February 13, 2018, https://www .aam-us.org/2018/02/13/new-national-data-reveals-the-economic-impact-of-muse ums-is-more-than-double-previous-estimates/.

2

Surveying Triumphs and Challenges

It is easy to call for prescriptive solutions that dictate the "right way" to achieve financial success, but this is presumptuous. Museums vary widely in scale and resources and have their own unique set of pressures, challenges, and limitations. What works for one may not work for another; each must work within its own individual circumstances. It is perhaps more instructive to paint a picture of the typical types of financial challenges that museums face, why they found themselves in these situations, and what they did to resolve them.

Research shows several recurring patterns of problematic financial issues in museums. Most common were 1) overly aggressive expansion; 2) limited revenue diversification; 3) lack of discipline and oversight; 4) limited ability to compete in changing times; and/or 5) lack of entrepreneurship. Organizations large and small experienced varying degrees of these issues. Some responded boldly and creatively (in some cases too boldly or even controversially); others worked to keep up with changing times for their very survival; many became more entrepreneurial to grow their revenue streams and sharpen their relevancy; and still others learned to take their financial oversight responsibilities more seriously.

RECOGNIZING PROBLEMS AND TAKING ACTION

Even museums on the verge of collapse bounced back and found their way to a more positive future by acknowledging their problems and refocusing programming, tightening operations, and making hard decisions. Sometimes it took an impending crisis to force action and secure the attention of leaders to acknowledge there was a serious financial issue. In many cases, there were warning signs well in advance, and often there was the hope that the financial storm would recede—perhaps the problem was only temporary and things would surely get better. Only emergency fixes along the way avoided complete collapse. Unfortunately, conditions often worsened, and the cumulative effect became so severe that some museums were pushed to the very brink of failure.

One Revolutionary War historic site in New England was on the verge of closing as a result of a funding crisis in early 2018 after eighty-seven years of operation. "We faced an existential challenge and had to make some decisions about how we could fundamentally change the organization for the better," noted its board chair. Museum trustees took decisive action and reduced operating costs; strengthened community ties by adding new board members; became more family focused; streamlined the management structure; eliminated some programs; and refocused others around the museum's core mission. As a result of these changes, the museum made itself more relevant, improved its programmatic activity, and better positioned itself for long-term financial viability.[1]

Another New England historic site very nearly closed its doors in 2008, when it found itself nearly $9 million in debt and in danger of foreclosure on its forty-acre property. According to the board of trustees, financial problems had plagued the site for years, and conditions had become so bad that it defaulted on a $2.6 million loan borrowed to purchase collections. Seven employees were laid off, and the museum missed a $30,000 loan payment to a local bank. The board, entirely new since 2006, acknowledged that it must immediately restructure and reorganize to "broaden and deepen the management structure, in terms of both fundraising and financial oversight."[2] The museum did just that and began a public fundraising campaign. As a result, financial conditions began to change, especially with the help of a number of targeted donors who retired the museum's entire debt. The museum continued to make great progress in ensuring its long-term sustainability, and it worked to grow an endowment that today totals over $8 million.[3]

One mid-sized art museum found itself slipping into a precarious financial position after funding dropped significantly over a period of five years, largely due to the loss of energy industry funding in its state. The museum experienced reduced support from state and city government, several foundation grants ended, and private donations were less robust because of a declining economy. Museum leaders recognized that they had to respond and began an aggressive initiative to diversify financial support. Their goal was to create a diversified funding base with more emphasis on business management, so that when the museum "hit these hard times we can keep going. . . . I think it's been time for the (museum) to do this for years," and "if we don't change and adapt, we won't survive," according to the board chair. The museum reorganized staffing to focus more on business management, marketing, social media, and memberships; developed an active event rental program; implemented tighter controls on its finances; implemented systems to better understand the overall financial picture; offered fee-for-service workshops; improved museum sales; and developed a series of special events. As a result of these changes, the museum director stated that they no longer "rely on any one particular source because at any given time that one source can go away. . . . 'I think we're on the right path.'"[4]

One of the most distinguished outdoor museums in the United States experienced significant financial challenges in recent years but took major steps to address them. In 2017, the president and CEO was forthcoming with these financial challenges in a letter to the public. He stated that the museum was spending more than necessary and dipping into the museum endowment far too often. He noted that it would have to make some "fundamental changes" or its endowment would all but disappear within eight years.

The museum had relied for decades on significant endowment income to help cover its operating expenses. In good economic times, endowment earnings were used to help fund operations, which is what the endowment was designed to do. But in bad economic times, the museum was forced not only to use endowment earnings but also to dip into endowment principal to sustain operations. This approach solved short-term problems, but it could not be the *modus operandi* moving forward because it reduced the potential for future endowment growth and income. Like many institutions, the museum's expenses continued to outpace operating revenues as it tried to maintain its much-acclaimed program and quality services while also trying to keep it affordable and accessible to the public. As a result, more and more funds were drawn from the endowment—a business model that was not sustainable because the endowment would eventually evaporate. As an example, between 2013 and 2016 the value of the endowment slid by approximately 15 percent as a result of continued withdrawals. Continued endowment draws would further erode this source of revenue and imperil the museum's future viability, especially in light of the national trend of declining attendance at museums of its type.

In its 2017 reaccreditation report by the American Alliance of Museums, it was noted that the museum's "financial health is fragile" and "is not yet able to meet its financial obligations without drawing down on its endowment in a way that is not sustainable." In response, the museum's strategic plan outlined significant changes to make it more fiscally sound.[5]

Museum leaders called upon the services of McKinsey & Company, Ernst & Young, and other business consultants to help it navigate a more sustainable future. Reducing overall expenditures; outsourcing much of its unprofitable commercial operations; reducing debt; and most importantly, decreasing reliance on endowment were keys to long-term sustainability and a new business model.[6] Today work continues on the museum's financial challenges as it makes difficult financial decisions, increases fundraising to unprecedented levels, and works to expand its services and programs. "We've built a plan to help strengthen our financial profile . . . and made good progress and are excited about where we are," said the CEO.[7]

BEING BOLD AND INNOVATIVE

Some museums took bold steps to become more relevant, reach broader audiences, and strengthen their bottom lines. In a time of scarce funding and keen competition, organizations looked at new ways to attract audiences and scrutinize the cost-benefit ratio of their activities.

The Santa Cruz Museum of Art & History significantly changed its approach to programming, and in 2011–2012 it reported attendance that *doubled in one year*, even with reduced staff and budget! This was largely due to a more aggressive and inclusive agenda of community programs. The museum sought out programs that its constituency wanted and actually created them. They defined specific target audiences and made programs available at predictable times. In addition, in an effort to involve more people and make programs more cost-effective, the museum partnered with numerous local artists and community organizations, who contributed their many talents, interests, and resources. Many program materials were donated, resulting in a typical program budget of less than $100! As a result, the museum became more relevant, increased attendance, and made its bottom line healthier. The overarching driver in the success was because they were, according to then–executive director Nina Simon, "shamelessly resourceful."[8]

In 2011 the Marine Museum in Fall River, Massachusetts, founded in 1968, fell on hard times. Largely a volunteer operation whose survival depended on the work of a core group of supporters, the museum struggled to survive with volunteers who had "to do everything . . . to make sure that the museum stays alive. It's a difficult thing to do," said the board chair, "to stay on top of something that has no employees." He noted that he and a few others were doing everything from maintaining the lawn and shoveling snow to raising money and welcoming visitors. The museum's prospects for survival were bleak.[9]

The museum resurrected itself in 2017 when it merged with Battleship Cove: America's Fleet Museum and rebranded itself as the Maritime Museum at Battleship Cove. The museum was reorganized; new staff were hired; upgrades were planned; and exhibits were installed. Museum traffic increased and the museum took on new life. The two organizations built upon each other's strengths, and both became stronger. In a happy ending to a difficult story, the Marine Museum successfully rebounded itself.[10]

BEING BOLD AND (PERHAPS) TOO AGGRESSIVE

Funding for museums has always been challenging, but the problem is often exacerbated by the need to improve programs and services. The lure of a new exhibition wing or building may seem like the answer to give the museum new life and provide a positive course correction for the future. These pressures sometimes encourage revenue projections that are overly optimistic and the downsides are not fully considered.

One major art museum found itself struggling with deficits nearing $40 million; massive layoffs of staff; postponement of a multimillion-dollar exhibition wing; reductions in its number of exhibitions; low institutional morale; and other issues. The museum's problems were caused in large part by an aggressive expansion program that included overspending on a new building; rebranding initiatives; borrowing heavily from the endowment to cover costs; and pursuing a new wing before solid financial plans and funding were in place. These issues were compounded by falling revenue in sales and admissions, as well as an ever-increasing rise in expenses. It was simply a question of doing too much too fast, according to many who felt museum leaders did not fully grasp the implications of aggressive expansion and its relationship to core programs, finances, and morale. There was concern that the museum was too heavily focused on expansion and not enough on emphasizing the programs that made the museum great in the first place.[11] In response to major revenue losses, caused in part by the pandemic, the museum scheduled the sale of collections to help raise funds for the care of its collections. "It seems appropriate to use the proceeds of our regular deaccessioning program to support salaries for collection care staff in this exceptional year," said the museum's director.[12]

One venerable natural history museum in the Midwest faced similar issues. In 2002 it issued $90 million worth of bonds (three times more than ever before) for various exhibitions; structural upgrade projects for a building nearly a century old; a new collections center; and a new entrance. These initiatives increased debt levels and added significantly to operational costs. The museum relied on overly optimistic revenue projections and believed that expansion would increase attendance and revenue. They had not secured pledges for nearly enough funding before beginning these projects and predicated their funding largely on investment returns they believed would exceed the costs of borrowing. By 2011 the museum had raised only about $150 million of the $254 million that it spent. As a result of the borrowing and the economic downturn of 2008, the museum was faced with major layoffs, fewer exhibitions, and reductions and the restructuring of museum operations, which according to one curator would "dramatically and permanently change the nature and mission" of the museum.

In an effort to protect their credit rating, the museum also borrowed $12 million to pay down debt. Museum leaders believed at the time that they were making prudent financial decisions, but the economy turned sour and financial projections did not meet expectations. As a result, they felt they had no options but to move forward with their initiatives to sustain visitation levels.[13]

Expansion is not confined to brick-and-mortar construction. One foundation, created to support a major historical museum and library, found itself struggling with a debt of $9.7 million as a result of a 2007 loan it took out to buy a collection of historical artifacts.[14] The foundation felt the collections were vitally important to the museum and wanted to seize the opportunity to acquire the objects. In addition, it wanted to keep the items in the public domain and not lose them forever into private hands. Despite donor fatigue from the newly developed library and museum, and lack of initial cash, the foundation believed the opportunity was of such importance that it decided to move ahead with the purchase.

The collection was purchased for $25 million ($23 million of which was borrowed), which the foundation expected to repay from private donations. Unfortunately, the foundation encountered difficulty raising funds to pay off the entire amount. They started a GoFundMe page,[15] and the museum even leased an important historical document for $50,000 to help pay down the debt.[16] The foundation also asked already financially strapped state lawmakers to help pay its loan debts in a desperate attempt to avoid selling off some of the very collections it had purchased![17]

After it stopped making significant payments on the loan, the foundation seriously considered auctioning some of the collection to help pay for its original purchase. Fortunately, the foundation received a three-year extension on its loan repayment terms, which allowed more time for repayment, but the entire episode severely hampered perceptions of the museum and the foundation's ability to raise additional money. Under the new terms of the loan, the foundation was expected to retire the debt by an extended deadline, and it looks forward "to the day when we can pay it off completely."[18]

Another major museum, like so many others driven to grow attendance, increase revenues, and stimulate economic activity in their cities, went deeply into debt to fund an aggressive and risky expansion program that did not meet financial projections. Burdened with $28 million in debt and debt service of around 10 percent of its operating budget, the museum pursued a program of opening museum stores across the state, purchased a half interest in an IMAX theater, and developed various major exhibitions. There were additional expenses to operate the expansion activity, such as increased staffing and utilities, as well as rising costs generally. Unfortunately, attendance remained flat, and the new retail and IMAX ventures lost $1.5 million. As a result, the museum ended the 2006 fiscal year with a $10 million deficit and only $387,000 left in its endowment. The museum simply fell victim to overexpansion and growth projections that did not materialize.[19]

Opening with great expectations of tourist traffic and associated economic activity, a southern maritime museum was forced to close thirteen months after it opened in 2015. The museum, a $62-million public-private initiative, was funded mostly from private donations with the city borrowing another $28 million. The museum soon found itself in an unsustainable financial position after it failed to reach attendance numbers in its very first year of operation. The city was forced to develop a "Corrective Action Plan" and completely rethink the museum's business model and management.[20]

Other museums were victims of overly aggressive expansion. Only two months after its grand opening, a newly developed museum in Washington, DC, announced that it would default on a portion of the $103 million in bonds that it had borrowed in 2016. The Museum had counted on the fundraising prowess of celebrity supporters and aggressive projections of anticipated attendance to fund operations. Unfortunately, the museum achieved only about 20 percent of its anticipated visitation. It had a difficult time competing in a city that boasts about 160 museums—many of which are free. The museum reported a net loss of $6.1 million in 2018, forcing it to raise ticket prices and reduce staff. Continued long-term operation of the museum became questionable.[21]

Museums that experienced problems in this category were not limited by institutional size, budget, discipline, or location. The trend—the need to capture new revenue, enthusiasm for expansion and growth, and the creation of new audiences—was consistent. While the projects were worthy, optimism was not always rewarded due to the realities of unexpected economic downturns; underestimated costs and overestimated fundraising, miscalculations about ongoing operational costs; or lack of careful planning for the realities of additional operational costs once the new facility opened. Many organizations had little option but to move forward—deals were struck, funds spent, public expectations high, donors committed—and turning back was not an option.

BEING BOLD BUT CONTROVERSIAL

Sometimes museums found themselves with limited options when facing desperate financial challenges. Drastic action was often necessary, although usually as a reluctant last resort. There were many reasons why museums found themselves in such positions. There may have been years of deferred infrastructure repair that could be deferred no longer; tight, precarious operating budgets prevented the growth of financial reserves to fund emergencies; depletion of endowments to cover years of operating deficits reduced an endowment's ability to earn income; the recognition that modernization and upgrading were necessary to maintain relevancy and appeal; growing costs of museum operations, including care of collections; the need to expand or improve facilities; interest in significantly increasing endowment; the economic impact of the pandemic; and the need to generally position the museum for the future. In the ideal world, museums would have planned for these eventualities, but pressures of day-to-day finances and operational survival were priorities and other matters often deferred and simply beyond consideration. The growth of financial demands were insidious with needs increasing over time until desperate action was forced. Certainly desperate, last-resort action was not a position any organization wished for, but institutions sometimes found themselves in this position with little choice but to act quickly, boldly, and even controversially.

In New England, trustees formulated a long-term plan for their museum that included reimagining the overall museum to make it more relevant, create a $40-million operating endowment, upgrade aging exhibitions, and make repairs to building infrastructure. Trustees felt the plan would stabilize museum finances and position it for a brighter future. The problem was that they proposed to fund the plan through the deaccessioning and sale of twenty-two works from the museum's collections. The proceeds would be used to fund projects unrelated to collections care or reacquisition and collided directly with ethical concerns raised by the museum profession.

The museum came under fire when the American Alliance of Museums (AAM) and the Association of Art Museum Directors (AAMD) criticized what was considered a violation of museum ethics in the museum's sale of the collection. Museum trustees, in turn, argued that the sale would allow the financially struggling museum to essentially save the museum for future generations and "protect our most important asset: our open doors."[22]

The AAM and AAMD, however, argued that it was inappropriate to use the funds for the purposes specified by the museum because such a sale would "undermine the public's trust in the mission of nonprofit museums" if collections were viewed as negotiable assets. And further, the sale would discourage fundraising activities as well as continued donations of works of art.[23]

The museum ultimately sold the works from its collection for $53.25 million after considerable public controversy, protests, and an agreement between the museum and the state attorney general with approval from the state supreme court.[24] The museum recently installed improved lighting; added several small "pocket" galleries, a freight elevator, flooring, and a sewer line; and waterproofed the building's foundation at a cost of $3.5 million, paid entirely from deaccessioning proceeds.[25]

In another instance, an art museum sold major works from its collections to fully pay down its construction debts of $19.8 million in order to avoid invading its endowment. According to the CEO of the museum, the sale was ultimately a question of keeping the museum open or drowning in a sea of debt and ultimately closing the museum. According to the CEO, "We reached our most important goal—keeping the museum open and thriving."[26]

In 2008 the AAMD censured a museum after it sold two Hudson River School paintings for $13.5 million to pay museum operating expenses. The museum planned to sell two more paintings to generate another $1.5 million in income for the same purposes, but after being censured, it decided instead to pursue more aggressive fundraising, better management/oversight of its finances, and a strategic planning process with a reconfigured board of trustees. According to one official, museum trustees had considered doing these things for years, but nothing had "ever been substantively done about them." The AAMD offered the expertise of its members to assist the museum on a volunteer basis.[27]

An art museum in California announced plans to liquidate its entire 1,600-work collection to provide the organization with more long-term financial stability. In response to a letter from sixty curators, artists, and dealers who objected to the sale, the museum director noted that the sale was necessary to "provide a sustainable future for the organization" and that "our decision to take this course of action was not made easily or lightly, and it is the only viable solution that will allow for the organization to continue to remain open."[28]

Not all proceeds from deaccessioning sales, however, were used for overtly non-collections-related expenses. In a controversial 1996 sale, the Shelburne Museum in Vermont sold twenty-two pieces from its collections, two-thirds of which had been in storage for years, and established a $25 million "Collections Care Endowment," the purpose of which was to develop a permanent source of funding for the care of its overall collection of eighty thousand items. The restricted endowment's income was to be used for collections-care expenses only and was expected to adhere to the institution's carefully defined parameters of what constituted "collections care." The decision to proceed was a difficult one for the museum, and after much study and analysis, it considered this approach to be a last resort "survival strategy to ensure that its collections were cared for."[29]

Collections of some university museums were not viewed as resources to support the mission of the museum, but rather to support the general programs of the university. As a result, universities took a number of approaches to generate revenue for programs unrelated to the museum. One university made a decision to sell a significant painting and use the proceeds to support the *college's* operating budget. The museum was sanctioned by the AAMD, which said that the proceeds of the sale would be "utilized for a purpose that we believe will, ultimately, be damaging to our field." The AAMD had previously censured the museum when it sold another painting for the same purpose.[30] At another university, an idea was floated to sell Jackson Pollock's *Mural* to pay for student scholarships. Advocates said that the sale of the painting, valued at $140 million, would give as many as one thousand students a full-ride scholarship every year.[31] At one museum in the East, officials put forth an idea to sell works from the university museum, not because it needed the funds to survive, but because it could more effectively use the money generated by the sale of forty-six artworks (valued by as much as $7.3 million) "for funding the university's new strategic five-year plan," according to a spokesperson. The museum was rebuked by both AAM and AAMD.[32]

Regardless of one's view of the ethical issues involved, examples such as these underscore the extreme pressure felt by organizations and their leaders to resort to desperate measures to make their institutions financially sustainable. Perhaps it was their own fault that their organizations found themselves in these positions and perhaps not, but they responded boldly, even if it meant brushing against standard ethical norms.

KEEPING UP WITH CHANGING TIMES

Museums adapted to changing times with varying degrees of success. Struggling with basic operating expenses, many smaller institutions found themselves in an untenable situation as they tried to respond to changing levels of visitor sophistication and interests.

Audiences have many leisure-time choices, and they expect museums to provide contemporary interactive exhibitions, interesting and meaningful programs, and unique and entertaining experiences. Yet the costs to keep pace with technology and changing visitor expectations compete with other fundamental museum priorities such as the need to fund ongoing operations, address aging and failing infrastructures, care for the collections, and many more. Museums must maintain a competitive edge for their very survival, but for many museums this has been impossible.

The Soldiers' National Museum in Gettysburg closed and its contents sold at auction in 2014 after over fifty years of operation because of the need "to stay relevant, and that's difficult with all the changing technology and expectations . . . and you have to keep making changes and look at different ways of doing things," noted the president of Gettysburg Tours, Inc. According to one sixty-four-year-old visitor who had visited many times, "I think people are looking for things that . . . jump out and grab you. Our children are too busy with things on computers and the Internet. Things like this (antiquated exhibitions) don't grab their attention." The prospects for the museum were not helped by the creation of the $103 million National Park Service Visitor Center, which boasted many high-tech features and a yearly visitation of over one million. In addition, the museum's fate was sealed by the new Gettysburg Seminary Ridge Museum, which was also outfitted with state-of-the-art exhibitions.[33]

Many small museums are founded by earnest and enthusiastic people who want to preserve some aspect of their community culture. They learn quickly that a museum enterprise is costly and complicated. Making the museum sustainable is no easy task, regardless of size. Small museums are particularly vulnerable because they often do not have the resources to be viable. The challenge for these organizations is that the bar has been set much higher than ever before. Today's audiences are far too sophisticated, and they demand more than a dimly lit room full of seemingly unrelated objects and faded photographs.[34]

In New York, the St. Lawrence County historian said that one of her key concerns is to "attract a younger audience and get them engaged." Many organizations face similar problems. They have limited funding with which to operate, barely covering utilities and other basic expenses. They make extensive use of volunteers, have limited hours of operation, tend to appeal to a decidedly older audience, and have no means or expertise to attract new audiences.

The Tupper Lake Heritage Museum in Tupper Lake, New York, housed at the old Junction Fire Station, faced closing in 2018 for safety code violations. The building, owned by the town of Tupper Lake, was shared with the local snowmobile club along with its equipment, which visitors had to walk through to get to both floors of the museum. The museum was largely a curiosity treasure chest of town history in a building faced with serious liability issues. The town was asked by its insurance carrier to close the building. The donation-funded museum had only $8,000 in cash reserves, and the possibility of improving the museum and increasing yearly attendance was unlikely. The museum, largely driven by the efforts of ten volunteers, opened only a few months each year. This story is typical of many small, local history museums in which a group of enthusiastic and well-meaning individuals, proud of their local heritage, have amassed a considerable collection with the hope of sharing it with the general public, but there is little support beyond the small group for the museum's long-term survival.[35]

In some instances, the ongoing financial viability of small institutions was imperiled even with significant investment by the government. The Georgia Music Hall of Fame, created in 1979 at a cost of $6.6 million, found itself struggling with low attendance (about 20 percent of projections), despite having an impressive collection and location in a region with great musical traditions (Allman Brothers, Ray Charles, Little Richard et al.).[36] The museum was located in Macon, Georgia, because legislators felt that too many cultural institutions were located in the Atlanta area and they wanted to invigorate the economy in more rural regions. But the Macon area was not a popular tourist destination, which created problems for attendance projections. The museum's ongoing survival was largely dependent upon increased state support and significant fundraising activity, neither of which happened. Unfortunately, the Hall was forced to close in 2011 due to lack of attendance. The collection was moved to the University of Georgia, and the Hall of Fame awards were moved to another venue.[37]

REBRANDING AND REINVIGORATING

There were a large number of museums who chose a strategy of rebranding to help keep pace in the marketplace by identifying themselves in a more current and appealing fashion. The strategy to rebrand helped send the message that an organization was changing—less antiquated and exclusive—and more inclusive, relevant, and exciting. As examples, the Colorado Historical Society became History Colorado and the Ohio Historical Society became the Ohio History Connection to "usher in the next evolving generation of historical preservation both live and online."[38] The Society for the Preservation of New England Antiquities was rebranded as Historic New England for similar reasons. According to the *Magazine Antiques*, the original name sounded too "fuddy-duddy."[39]

Rebranding helped redefine institutions as more lively and contemporary to attract new audiences, underscore their continued relevance, and remind visitors they still offered important cultural resources and experiences. Naturally there was always the hope that all of this would also add to the bottom line. The Henry Ford Museum changed its name to the Henry Ford Museum of American Innovation as a result of its desire to "better serve our visitors," according to the museum's president.[40] The San Diego Museum of

Man changed its name to the Museum of Us to "better reflect our values of inclusivity, equity, and love; [it] better describes all the people we serve and the stories we want to tell; and [it] fully embodies our mission of inspiring human connections by exploring the human experience."[41] And, among others, the Adirondack Museum became the Adirondack Experience, the Craft & Folk Art Museum became Craft Contemporary, the Newark Museum became the Newark Museum of Art, the Virginia Historical Society rebranded as the Virginia Museum of History and Culture, and the Mesa Southwest Museum became the Arizona Museum of Natural History.

SEARCHING FOR DIVERSIFICATION

Many museums survive on a patchwork of funding sources that together provide a precarious existence even in the best of times. Even the smallest downward slip in revenues has crippling consequences, especially if museums are over-reliant on only a few (or even one) significant funding source(s). And when a major funding source is reduced or eliminated, the crisis becomes existential in nature. There are often no reserve funds, no endowment, and no generous public entity willing to bail them out.

The Philadelphia History Museum closed in 2018 after years of struggling to find a mix of sustainable funding. The 100,000-object museum, situated in a building built in 1826 and located near the Liberty Bell, received city support "in a significant way, for years" according to the city's managing director. Unfortunately, city support, the major source of funding for the museum, was reduced and more reductions planned. There was hope that the museum would partner with Temple University and a more sustainable business model would emerge. Unfortunately, after much consideration Temple decided "not to pursue an alliance with the Philadelphia History Museum at this time," according to the dean of libraries at Temple. Previous talks about a partnership or merger a few years earlier with the Woodmere Art Museum also were unsuccessful. The Philadelphia History Museum, without major support from the city, had no choice but to close its doors for at least six months while it contemplated what to do.[42] It has since determined that it will transfer its collections to Drexel University.[43]

The Northwest Museum of Arts and Culture in Spokane closed its historic 1897 Campbell House when state funding was reduced by 50 percent, although it planned to remain open for school groups. Hopes were that if funding was restored, the museum would reopen during subsequent fiscal years.[44] Currently the site is open for self-guided tours on a limited basis.[45]

The Panhandle-Plains Historical Museum in Canyon, Texas, is the largest historical museum in Texas and is located on the campus of West

Texas A&M University. In 2018–2019, the museum faced a 30 percent state budget cut and another 30 percent reduction slated for the subsequent year. The museum compensated for the revenue shortfall and relied on public support to come to its rescue. It raised more than $160,000 and expected to host a major black-tie gala and fundraising events for each of the next five years. The community seemed determined to save the ninety-eight-year-old museum. According to one museum official, "We're not going anywhere," and "we are already planning our 100th birthday." The museum planned to survive just as it did during the dark days of the Great Depression when the community came to its aid.[46] The museum has seemingly recovered from these financial threats, continues to offer a full slate of services and programs and has an active fundraising program.[47]

Common were stories such as the temporary closing of the Haskell Indian Nations University Cultural Center and Museum in Lawrence, Kansas. The museum featured exhibitions from archival and artifact collections, as well as Native American and student artwork.[48] The organization, with its collections dating to 1884, lost the grant it relied on to operate and closed indefinitely as it pursued new funding sources.[49] University officials were confident that the museum would ultimately resume operating, and it has since reopened.

The Chanute Air Museum in Rantoul, Illinois, closed after the Village of Rantoul asked the museum to pay a greater share of its operating costs. The village could no longer afford to fund most of the museum's operating costs of approximately $10,000 per month and other growing expenses of the museum. The museum needed 6,500 visitors per month without village support, which made ongoing operation impossible. The museum, which opened in 1994, could not make up the funding gap left by the village and was forced to close. Its collections and exhibitions were distributed to other museums.[50]

WATCHING THE STORE

Embezzlement has become a common crime in nonprofits generally, and museums have not been exempt from this trend. Many crimes were prosecuted, and news stories made the broader museum profession more aware of their own vulnerability. This has resulted in the tightening of financial controls at many institutions, but it is often the case that such changes in financial practice are put in place after damage has been done.

Museums are built on high levels of trust among trustees, staff, and volunteers. This is especially true in organizations that do not have the means or expertise to properly monitor their resources. Sometimes trust is misplaced and results in serious issues even in the largest and most highly monitored financial operations. Sometimes those who are comfortable in their positions know the vulnerabilities of a museum's financial protocols and are tempted at the relative ease of stealing. In other cases, staff members feel justified in stealing because they view the museum as "owing" them because of low salaries in the field. Regardless of the motivation, administrators must take measures to minimize the possibility of theft and provide a strong program of checks and balances. This extends to the handling of all museum resources, regardless of how trustworthy they perceive a staff member.

Careless financial procedures and a lack of oversight frequently encourage such illicit conduct. According to the director of one museum in Virginia (his own museum a victim of embezzlement by a staff member), "Unfortunately, you trust people to be of a high level of integrity, and at times, whether you have that or not, things happen." In the case of his museum, an employee was dismissed immediately for stealing and the issue turned over to police. Audits then identified loose financial practices by the museum that have since been corrected.[51]

The chief financial officer of a New England museum managed to steal over $1 million over a period of six years by creating credit card accounts for herself and family members. She used the cards to pay for such personal expenses as college tuition for her children. She manipulated the books to make it look as though the charges were legitimate museum expenses. She was charged with seventeen counts of larceny and credit card fraud and another for making false corporate entries. The museum president noted that, "This whole process clarified a number of things for us. I feel we have a far better understanding of our finances, and we're safer than we were before." After the museum brought the suit against the staff member, it stated that it would take steps to institute tighter financial controls.[52]

One of the more spectacular embezzlement schemes took place nearly thirty years ago at a major California museum when a deputy director, chief financial officer, and secretary were charged with embezzling $2.1 million between 1988 and 1994. The trio used museum funds to purchase cars and jewelry and pay down personal debts. They stole government funds, ticket proceeds, and private donations. According to the deputy district attorney, "You had only one person looking over the purse strings (referring to the deputy director), a person in whom they had extreme confidence. He had control over the books, and no one was looking over his shoulder. And that's a perfect recipe for theft." Money was channeled into investment accounts, cashier's checks were written to the secretary, accounts were opened in the museum's name without the museum's approval, and large sums of money were deposited in personal accounts. Amounts got progressively larger as time went on and the trio felt increasingly comfortable. The crimes were noticed when the museum's new director noticed discrepancies as he worked to tighten the museum financial controls. All three individuals were charged, and the deputy director faced charges of grand theft, misuse of public money, money laundering, and conspiracy.[53]

At a smaller Massachusetts museum, the thirty-six-year-old business manager embezzled hundreds of thousands of dollars between 2012–2015 by failing to deposit cash receipts and issuing unauthorized payments to herself from museum accounts. She faced a sentence of up to twenty years in prison, significant fines, and restitution.[54]

At a large Midwestern museum, a data records supervisor in the membership department pled guilty to stealing more than $400,000 from the museum, although federal authorities believe the amount was over $900,000. Having worked at the museum in several different positions from 2003–2014, she admitted keeping cash that patrons paid to the museum for ticket sales and cocktails purchased during special functions. The museum immediately put into place a much more stringent cashhandling procedure.[55]

In 2009 an accountant at an Arizona museum, who had worked at the museum since 1990, was indicted on three counts of fraudulent schemes and artifices, three counts of theft, and one count of illegally conducting an enterprise. Each count was a felony. The accountant was accused of embezzling $973,010 from the museum by forging the signature of the museum's chief financial officer and director, stealing cash from the museum store intended for deposits, and manipulating the general ledger to hide her activities. The wrongdoing was uncovered during the museum's internal audit.[56]

Smaller museums were also prone to various forms of illicit activity. The museum board of a small museum in North Carolina was "shocked" when the museum's curator (the only paid employee) was charged with one count of felony embezzlement. The trusted curator, who had no prior record other than being charged with one speeding ticket and driving with an expired vehicle registration, was not a likely subject for a major criminal charge. Between credit cards and cash, however, approximately $70,000 was stolen from the museum during the years 2010–2014—a large amount of money considering the museum's modest operating budget. The thefts were discovered when museum trustees noticed discrepancies in the museum's finances, which they immediately reported to the authorities. The local police chief noted that, "It can happen anywhere from convenience stores to a large store. You'd be surprised when and where money gets stolen, or the kinds of people who would steal."[57]

Even a tiny museum in Michigan was victim of two counts of embezzlement when its director, who had served in her position for more than fourteen years, was charged with two counts of embezzlement and three counts of forgery with reported losses in excess of $20,000. According to a news article, until the employee was terminated, she "was considered absolutely trustworthy" by the museum's board of directors.[58]

NOT JUST IN THE UNITED STATES

It is not just museums in the United States that have financial challenges. In Australia, the Castlemaine Art Museum was in danger of closing when it lost major funding, but at the last minute an anonymous donor came forward with a private gift of $250,000 to help save, at least temporarily, the century-old museum. In 2015 a report noted that the museum's financial condition had been "precarious for many years." Sotheby's Australia helped facilitate the gift. The couple who gave the gift suggested that funding might continue in the future, but it depended "on the level of support and engagement from the community as a whole." While the museum was saved for the moment, its future is still uncertain.[59]

In London, the Type Museum, which told the story of the evolution of type design and manufacture, closed after fourteen years of operation. The reason for the closing was that the museum "had been unable to secure core funding." Their hope was to find a source of funding to continue the ongoing support for the museum, but it seemed unlikely.[60]

And in Beirut, Lebanon, the Sursock Museum, a popular modern art museum, closed its doors on Mondays as a result of financial issues related to the struggling Lebanon economy. The museum was free to the public, because it did not want to make "access to culture more difficult," according to the museum director. The museum hoped to reopen on Mondays if it could find $100,000 per year to support doing so. The hope was to obtain funds from the Ministry of Culture of Lebanon, but it seemed unlikely.[61]

The Big Idea Centre in Scotland was an interactive museum of Scottish invention that opened in 2000 and designed to be self-supporting through admissions. The founders were determined to operate the museum without public subsidy. The museum was forced to close when attendance projections were not realized and there was no adequate, ongoing funding. The chairman of the Centre noted that "I was determined to prove we could operate a science centre without public subsidy, but I failed. There is not a single science centre which operates without it."[62] The Centre closed in 2003. Much of the blame was attributed to its location on the site of Alfred Nobel's dynamite factory and the difficulty of access to the museum (past several miles of a live explosive factory)! Not only did the museum not have diversified funding, but it was developed under the notion that admissions would make it sustainable—a gamble that failed.

SUMMARY

Research suggests that most museums work to operate in a reasonable and fiscally responsible fashion but still face financial challenges. Many are successfully entrepreneurial, but even they are not exempt from falling victim to financial crises. Most wrestle with daily attendance and admissions numbers, nervously await store and café receipts, and eagerly hope for approval of funding requests. They take their financial responsibilities seriously; budget carefully; monitor financial statements and cash-flow reports regularly; and adjust spending when necessary. They generally manage according to reasonably sound financial practices.

Well-meaning and hardworking museums sometimes fall victim to financial crises for many different reasons. Sometimes trust is misplaced; finances are not given proper attention; organizations become complacent; management resources are limited; and expansion is not carefully considered, among other reasons. Yet others are able to manage these crises or avoid them altogether by putting systems in place, monitoring finances regularly, and taking decisive action.

ORGANIZATIONS THAT ENJOY SUCCESS:

Value planning, carefully monitor finances, and act before conditions are at a critical or irrevocable stage.

Carefully consider financial decisions, are relatively conservative with financial projections, and grow organically and not exponentially.

Recognize that change is constant and necessary to survive, and that educated, calculated risks are necessary.

Create an entrepreneurial culture throughout the organization.

Effectively manage a careful balance of money and mission.

Effectively manage the variables within their control and get the most from existing resources.

Develop a range of revenue streams without being overly dependent on only a few.

Blend short-term actions with long-term planning and always think of the future implications of immediate decisions.

NOTES

1. "Knox Museum in Thomaston in Turnaround Mode," knoxmuseum.org, February 14, 2018, http://knoxmuseum.org/news/knox-museum-in-turnaround-mode/.
2. Ellen G. Lahr, "Mount Leader steps down," *Berkshire Eagle*, March 31, 2008, https://www.berkshireeagle.com/stories/mount-leader-steps-down,105890.

3. Michelle Dean, "The fight to save Edith Wharton's beloved home from itself," *Guardian*, October 18, 2015, https://www.theguardian.com/books/2015/oct/18/fight-save-edith-wharton-home-the-mount.

4. Elysia Conner, "Nicolaysen Art Museum makes tough choices to survive during tough economic times," *Casper Star Tribune*, March 31, 2018, https://trib.com/news/local/casper/nicolaysen-art-museum-makes-tough-choices-to-survive-during-tough/article_d9da5d28-2287-57a2-afb7-c8d9f29ebc0a.html.

5. Robert Brauchle, "Debt, endowment drawdown threaten Colonial Williamsburg's long-term financial health," *Virginia Gazette*, October 17, 2017, https://www.dailypress.com/virginiagazette/news/va-vg-colonial-williamsburg-endowment-spending-20170919-story.html.

6. Kimberly Pierceall, "Colonial Williamsburg's CEO blamed past decisions for its dire state. But some of the most costly have been made under him," *Virginian-Pilot*, August 3, 2017, https://www.pilotonline.com/business/consumer/article_f94e25ed-5bb5-527c-a108-a2862ee3a1df.html.

7. Elizabeth Cooper, "History in the Making," *Virginia Business*, April 27, 2021, https://www.virginiabusiness.com/article/history-in-the-making/.

8. Nina Simon, "How We Doubled Our Attendance in a Year: One More Post About How Events Changed Our Attendance," *Museum 2.0*, July 18, 2012, http://museumtwo.blogspot.com/2012/07/how-we-doubled-attendance-in-year-one.html.

9. Michael Holtzman, "Marine Museum's finance, management issues worry founders," *Herald News*, July 31, 2011, https://www.heraldnews.com/x555032066/Marine-Museums-finance-management-issues-worry-founders.

10. Kevin P. O'Connor, "Battleship Cove, Marine Museum announce merger," *Herald News*, January 23, 2017, https://www.heraldnews.com/news/20170123/battleship-cove-marine-museum-announce-merger.

11. Robin Pogrebin, "Is the Met Museum 'a Great Institution in Decline'," *New York Times*, February 4, 2017, https://www.nytimes.com/2017/02/04/arts/design/met-museum-financial-troubles.html.

12. Angelica Villa, "Met to Sell $1 M. in Multiples to Raise Funds amid Budget Shortfall," ARTnews.com (ARTnews.com, September 20, 2021), https://www.artnews.com/art-news/market/metropolitan-museum-of-art-deaccessioning-multiples-1234604319/.

13. Heather Gillers and Jason Grotto, "Dinosaur-size Debt," *Chicago Tribune*, March 8, 2013, https://www.chicagotribune.com/news/ct-xpm-2013-03-08-ct-met-field-museum-debt-20130308-story.html.

14. Ben Szalinski, "Abraham Lincoln Presidential Library and Museum Cuts Ties with Foundation," *State Journal-Register*, April 1, 2021, https://www.sj-r.com/story/news/2021/04/01/lincoln-presidential-library-museum-ends-relationship-library-foundation/4841646001/.

15. Meagan Flynn, "Abe Lincoln's Library faces so much debt that it's considering selling his stuff—including his hat and gloves," *Chicago Tribune*, August 17, 2018, https://www.washingtonpost.com/news/morning-mix/wp/2018/08/17/abe-lincolns-library-faces-so-much-debt-its-considering-selling-his-stuff-including-his-hat-and-gloves/.

16. Brian Boucher, "A Whistleblower Busted the Lincoln Museum for Improperly Renting a Copy of the Gettysburg Address to Glenn Beck for $50,000," *Artnet News*, November 26, 2019, https://news.artnet.com/art-world/glenn-beck-1716267.

17. Mike Riopell, "Lincoln Museum Foundation Pleads for State Money to Avoid Selling Off Historic Artifacts," *Chicago Tribune*, May 15, 2019, https://www.chicagotribune.com/politics/ct-met-abe-lincoln-hat-hearing-20181113-story.html.

18. Association of Registrars and Collection Speialists, "Lincoln Artifacts Will Not Be Auctioned, Foundation Announces after Loan Extension," ARCS, accessed October 31, 2021, https://www.arcsinfo.org/news-events/entry/4120/lincoln-artifacts-will-not-be-auctioned-foundation-announces-after-loan-extension.

19. Stephanie Strom, "A Struggle for Solvency at Milwaukee Museum," *New York Times*, January 29, 2006, https://www.nytimes.com/2006/01/29/us/a-struggle-for-solvency-at-milwaukee-museum.html.

20. J.B. Biunno, "GulfQuest Maritime Museum Closing to Public Due to Low Attendance, Financial Woes," *WKRG News*, November 4, 2016, https://www.wkrg.com/news/gulfquest-maritime-museum-closing-to-public-due-to-low-attendance-financial-woes/.

21. Amanda Albright, "Richard Belzer and Clint Eastwood Can't Save the Failing National Law Enforcement Museum," *Bloomberg Businessweek*, March 18, 2019, https://www.bloomberg.com/news/articles/2019-03-18/richard-belzer-and-clint-eastwood-can-t-save-the-failing-national-law-enforcement-museum.

22. Jeff Jacoby, "The Berkshire Museum defends its most important asset: its open doors," *Boston Globe*, January 27, 2018, https://www.bostonglobe.com/opinion/2018/01/27/the-berkshire-museum-defends-its-most-important-asset-its-open-doors/M92tisiPanIT93ZHXKysCP/story.html.

23. "Statement on The Berkshire Museum Proposal to Deaccession Works of Art for Its Endowment, Operations, and to Fund Capital Investments," AAM press release, July 25, 2017, https://www.aam-us.org/2017/07/25/statement-on-the-berkshire-museum-proposal-to-deaccession-works-of-art-for-its-endowment-operations-and-to-fund-capital-investments/.

24. "Berkshire Museum completes controversial deaccessioning sales," *Apollo: The International Art Magazine*, November 28, 2018, https://www.apollo-magazine.com/berkshire-museum-completes-controversial-deaccessioning-sales/.

25. Larry Parnass and Screenshot by Larry Parnass—*The Berkshire Eagle*, "Berkshire Museum Invests $3.5m to Protect Building, Transform Pittsfield Mission," *Berkshire Eagle*, January 27, 2021, https://www.berkshireeagle.com/news/local/berkshire-museum-invests-3-5m-to-protect-building-transform-pittsfield-mission/article_cb61a4e8-6039-11eb-a8ba-f7a5c0a1689e.html.

26. Randy Kennedy, "Delaware Art Museum Completes Sale of Artworks to Repay Debt," Arts Beat: The New York Times, June 30, 2015, https://artsbeat.blogs.nytimes.com/2015/06/30/delaware-art-museum-completes-sale-of-artworks-to-repay-debt/.

27. Robin Pogrebin, "National Academy Revises Its Policies," New York Times, March 13, 2009, https://www.nytimes.com/2009/03/14/arts/design/14acad.html.

28. Alex Greenberger, "'An Irretrievable Loss': In Open Letter, Artists, Curators, Dealers Decry Selling Off of diRosa Foundation Holdings," ARTNews, August 20, 2019, http://www.artnews.com/2019/08/20/dirosa-foundation-open-letter/.

29. Brian Alexander, "Controversy and Collections," in History News (AASLH, 1998, Volume 53, #2), 21–24.
30. "Association of Art Museum Directors' Statement on Randolph College and Maier Museum of Art," *Association of Art Museums' Directors*, March 12, 2014, https://aamd.org/for-the-media/press-release/association-of-art-museum-direc tors-statement-on-randolph-college-and.
31. Kyle Chayka, "What's Going On with University of Iowa's Pollock?" *Hyperallergic*, February 21, 2011, https://hyperallergic.com/19092/university-of-iowa-pollock/.
32. Ellen Kinsella, "Outrage Mounts as LaSalle University Forges Ahead with Plan to Sell Works from Museum's Collection," ArtNet, January 5, 2018, https://news.artnet .com/art-world/la-salle-university-decision-to-deaccession-artworks-sparks-out rage-1193042.
33. Chris Kaltenbach, "After 50-plus years, Gettysburg's Soldier's National Museum is a goner," *Baltimore Sun*, November 1, 2014, https://www.baltimoresun.com/travel /bs-ae-museum-20141101-story.html.
34. W.T. Eckert and Olivia Belanger, "Small north country museums struggle to stay afloat," NNY360, September 3, 2018, https://www.nny360.com/news/small-north -country-museums-struggle-to-stay-afloat/article_c8e302ac-f879-5f32-8614 -3c21409df136.html.
35. Aaron Cerbone, "Tupper museum needs renovation," *Adirondack Daily Enterprise*, June 20, 2018, https://www.adirondackdailyenterprise.com/news/local-news/2018/06 /tupper-museum-needs-renovation/.
36. Jennifer Brett, "Georgia Music Hall of Fame in Trouble," *Atlanta Journal-Constitution*, July 24, 2009, https://www.ajc.com/entertainment/music/georgia-music-hall-fame -trouble/k5btXt4z7AiKkFiNdheFMJ/.
37. "Georgia Music Hall of Fame Museum and Education," Georgia Music Hall and Education Resources, accessed September 31, 2019, www.gamusichall.com/.
38. Ohio History Connection, Newsroom, April 2014, https://www.ohiohistory.org /about-us/newsroom/april-2014/ohio-history/connection-announcement.
39. Editorial Staff, "Celebrating the exotic and the ordinary," *Magazine Antiques*, January 7, 2010, https://www.themagazineantiques.com/article/laurel-thatchter-ulrich -and-historic-new-england/.
40. Daniel Strohl, "Henry Ford Museum changes its name to reflect focus on innovation," *Hemmings*, January 30, 2017, https://www.hemmings.com/blog/2017/01/30 /henry-ford-museum-changes-its-name-to-reflect-focus-on-innovation/.
41. San Diego Museum of Man, press release, July 27, 2018.
42. Jacey Fortin, "The Philadelphia History Museum Is Closing Its Doors (Maybe for Good)," *New York Times*, June 30, 2018, https://www.nytimes.com/2018/06/30/us /philadelphia-history-museum-close.html.
43. "The Philadelphia History Museum," Philadelphia History Museum, http://www .philadelphiahistory.org/.
44. Jim Kershner, "Spokane museum to close historic mansion after funding is cut," *Seattle Times*, November 7, 2008, https://www.seattletimes.com/life/travel/spokane -museum-to-close-historic-mansion-after-funding-is-cut/.
45. "Campbell House: Experience Spokane in the Early 1900s," Northwest Museum of Arts and Culture, accessed January 9, 2022, https://www.northwestmuseum.org /exhibitions/campbell-house/.

46. Aubrey McCall, "The Panhandle-Plains Historical Museum given a chance to prosper amid financial crisis," KFDA News, January 31, 2019, https://www.newschannel10.com/2019/01/31/panhandle-plains-historical-museum-given-chance-prosper-amid-financial-crisis/.

47. "Panhandle-Plains Historical Museum," Panhandle-Plains Historical Museum, accessed January 9, 2022, https://www.panhandleplains.org/.

48. "Haskell Indian Nations University Cultural Center," Kansas Tourism, accessed October 31, 2021, https://www.travelks.com/listing/haskell-indian-nations-university-cultural-center/2830/.

49. "Haskell Cultural Center and Museum to close indefinitely," AP NEWS, February 23, 2019, https://www.apnews.com/23c8b7795d3143f1a796ff21582c3c07.

50. Dave Hinton, "Chanute Air Museum closing in Rantoul," Ford County Record, April 23, 2015, https://www.fordcountyrecord.com/news/chanute-air-museum-closing-in-rantoul/article_c706601c-3c52-5d7d-808b-5db94f907428.html.

51. "Audit Shows Flaws in Museum Marred by Embezzlement," NBC29 WVIR-TV, August 15, 2013, https://www.nbc29.com/story/23022722/audit-shows-flaws-in-museum-marred-by-embezzlement.

52. Bruce S. Trachtenberg, "Fraud in Fruitlands-Museum Comes Late to Financial Controls," Nonprofit Quarterly, May 7, 2010, https://nonprofitquarterly.org/nonprofit-newswire-fraud-in-fruitlandsmuseum-comes-late-to-financial-controls/.

53. John M. Glionna, "3 Charged in Embezzlement at L.A. Museum," Los Angeles Times, July 13, 1995, https://www.latimes.com/archives/la-xpm-1995-07-13-mn-23539-story.html.

54. "Former Museum Business Manager Pleads Guilty to Wire Fraud," The United States Attorney's Office, District of Massachusetts, April 27, 2018, https://www.justice.gov/usao-ma/pr/former-museum-business-manager-pleads-guilty-wire-fraud.

55. Steve Johnson, "Former Field Museum employee admits to embezzling more than $400K," Chicago Tribune, January 4, 2016, https://www.chicagotribune.com/entertainment/museums/ct-field-museum-embezzling-pleads-guilty-story.html.

56. "Tucson Museum Accountant Charged in $973,000 Embezzlement," Arizona Attorney General Mark Brnovich Press Release, May 4, 2009, https://azag.gov/press-release/tucson-museum-accountant-charged-973000-embezzlement.

57. David Eldridge, "A Museum's True Colors," Macon County News, July 12, 2018, https://themaconcountynews.com/a-museums-true-colors/.

58. Brian Cabell, "Former Maritime Museum Director Arraigned," Word on the Street, April 8, 2016, https://wotsmqt.com/former-maritime-museum-director-arraigned/.

59. "A $250,000 anonymous donation has saved Victoria's Castlemaine Art Museum from closure," Business Insider Australia, August 3, 2017, https://www.businessinsider.com/a-250000-anonymous-donation-has-saved-victorias-castlemaine-art-museum-from-closure-2017-8.

60. Felicity Heywood, "Lack of funds lead to closure of London's Type Museum," Museums Journal, July 2006, https://www.museumsassociation.org/museums-journal/news/14864.

61. Emmanuel Khoury, "Cash-strapped Sursock Museum is looking for donors," L'Orient Le Jour, February 20, 2019, https://www.lorientlejour.com/article/1158179/cash-strapped-sursock-museum-is-looking-for-donors.html.

62. Amy Watson, "The Big Idea: Scotland's millennium project doomed to fail," Scotsman, August 9, 2016, https://www.scotsman.com/lifestyle-2-15039/the-big-idea-scotland-s-millennium-project-doomed-to-fail-1-4198151.

3

Blending Money and Mission

The COVID-19 pandemic profoundly affected the lives of millions of people. It also impacted the way museums conducted business and raised questions about their very survival. The American Alliance of Museums (AAM) predicted there would be "dire economic harm" to museums as a lasting effect of the virus, and initially estimated that the financial devastation caused by the virus would likely result in the "permanent closure of 12,000 museums" in the United States.[1]

The pandemic forced many museums into an existential crisis and resulted in two seismic shifts that forever changed the museum landscape. The first is that many museums will never recover from the devastating impact of the pandemic. Organizations with few or no financial reserves suffered from sustained periods of extreme financial hardship, and permanent closure seemed inevitable. The second major shift is that the pandemic forced museums to fundamentally reassess the way they work. Creative new approaches were conceived to conduct continued engagement with audiences while entrepreneurial energy was simultaneously unleashed to optimize resources and generate entirely new revenue streams.

Peter Drucker (1909–2005), described by *Business Week* as "the man who invented management," believed that difficult times are exactly when service organizations are at their most creative in finding solutions.[2] Drucker was convinced that "Most innovations in public service institutions are imposed on them either by outsiders or by catastrophe." He noted that willingly stopping what has always been done, risking precious resources, and trying something new is "excruciatingly painful" for service organizations because dramatic change requires experimentation and risk-taking, implies that pursuit of organizational mission is not being met, and forces organizations to reallocate carefully guarded financial and staff resources.[3]

Drucker cited as an example his view that the "greatest innova-tive thinking" in modern political history was the creation of the New Deal of 1933–1936. He noted that the New Deal was "triggered by a Depression so severe as almost to unravel the country's social fabric"—but for an entrepreneur, who "always searches for change, responds to it, and exploits it as an opportunity," conditions such as these present themselves as entrepreneurial possibilities.[4] Circumstances demanded that traditions be shed, risks be taken, and innovative problem-solving be employed.

Between the traditional struggles for funding and the pandemic, museums had no choice but to find opportunities in the crisis. In his remarks at the Cooperstown Graduate Program, secretary of the Smithsonian Institution Lonnie Bunch noted that "the pandemic forces us . . . to think about new revenue models, new business sources . . . and to collaborate more effectively."[5]

Crises demand resourcefulness and new ways of looking at things, but entrepreneur Daymond John reminds us that two other ingredients are essential for success. John, founder of the hip-hop fashion brand FUBU and investor-panelist on television's *Shark Tank* series, notes that to succeed, there must also be a desire to be "flat-out determined to get where you're going no matter what" and there must be a commitment to actually *do something*—create, experiment, test, prototype, and refine—and know that some failure is part of the process of finding solutions. Otherwise, he ad-vises, "Broke, on its own, is just broke."[6]

THE GROWING NEED FOR NEW APPROACHES

The pandemic forced museums to quickly adapt to travel and public assembly restrictions that threatened their very existence. Virtual expe-riences of all manner quickly became the order of the day as museums provided a way to stay connected to audiences and generate at least some revenue during a time of mandated closings and extreme operational chal-lenges. Many institutions created fundamentally new approaches to stay on their audience's radar while others developed more modest remedies or simply enhanced existing activities to meet their new challenges.

Institutions explored new ways of creating both cultural capital (staying connected and relevant to audiences) and financial capital (gener-ating income). Those that were unable to do so shuttered their doors and jeopardized their programmatic and financial lifelines. As Drucker predicted, an existential crisis forced service organizations like museums into becom-ing increasingly creative to meet their programmatic and financial needs. Some museums, however—such as the Indianapolis Museum of Art and its rebranding as "Newfields"; Old Sturbridge Village and the development of its charter school and contractual agreements to manage other historic sites; the Strong National Museum of Play and its "Neighborhood of Play" downtown revitalization project; and the Nelson-Atkins Museum initiative to develop a cultural district in downtown Kansas City—had developed major new initiatives long before the pandemic.

Although the pandemic is the most recent driver of new approaches in museums, it is not the only one. In their book *Enterprising Nonprofits*, authors J. Gregory Dees, Jed Emerson, and Peter Economy note the increased necessity of nonprofit leaders embracing entrepreneurship. They offer several compelling reasons, all of which apply to museums. These include the trend of reduced government funding; the growing complexity and requirements of operating a nonprofit organization; increased competition with the for-profit sector; questions about the effectiveness of traditional giving approaches; the demand by corporations for strategic benefits to their giving; and demands for performance measures by foundations.[7] These challenges are exacerbated by museums' growing funding needs for infrastructure repair, incorporation of new technologies, and the ever-increasing sophistication and expectations of audiences.

The need is also driven by the importance of diversifying revenue sources, a lesson learned in dramatic fashion during the financial crisis of 2008. Many museums that were heavily dependent on too few revenue sources suffered significant setbacks when that revenue was lost because of significant stock market declines. There was no way of replacing significant lost income because of their lack of diversified revenue streams.

Complicating matters is that nonprofit museums must carefully guard the manner in which they produce revenue because of a desire to protect their integrity and credibility. Considered by the American public to be "the most trustworthy source of information in America," every museum understandably wants to protect these important assets.[8] Many moneymaking initiatives are potentially profitable, but they may flirt with being mission-inappropriate and forever damage the museum's reputation. Instead, museums must balance their revenue initiatives with their mission imperatives in order to maintain institutional integrity. This, of course, is a delicate and difficult balance, because under budgetary duress, it is tempting to be swayed by revenue opportunities and lose sight of why the museum exists in the first place. But it does not have to be an either-or proposition.

Social entrepreneur Jerr Boschee writes that "Inspired vision, impassioned leadership, enthusiastic volunteers, government subsidies and a phalanx of donors are not always enough."[9] Today it takes creativity, innovation, risk-taking, and an institutional culture that nurtures experimentation and has the courage to change—or, in a word, entrepreneurship.

WHAT IS ENTREPRENEURSHIP EXACTLY?

Museums are showing signs of entrepreneurship on a wide scale, but what exactly does this mean? Entrepreneurship is a term often used, but sometimes misunderstood. Because the word is often associated with for-profit businesses, it sometimes suggests unrestrained commercialism with little room for the altruistic goals of museums. Stereotypes of entrepreneurs include those who take perilous risks, spend freely, and use investor capital to pursue initiatives that are not always carefully tested or planned in order to get the new product or service to commercial markets as quickly as possible. These individuals, according to Drucker, are the entrepreneurs who are *not* successful.[10]

In actuality, most successful entrepreneurs are those who minimize risks and engage in "hard, organized, and purposeful work."[11] They are the ones who stay "close to the customer" and know that if you don't "understand the customer, you won't understand the business."[12] They exercise a "rise and grind" work ethic and willingly do the daily drudgery necessary to succeed.[13] They are obsessed with testing and prototyping and live by the motto "ready, fire, aim." They embrace a fail-early-and-fail-often mentality.[14] Entrepreneurs know that success is dependent not just on innovation but on building *value* around the innovation—brilliant ideas by themselves aren't worth much if they don't meet a need or no one cares. Entrepreneurs optimize resources and competitive advantages and are willing to look at things in new ways, develop bold ideas, and work purposely to achieve them. And they embrace failures as opportunities to better understand how to fine-tune products or services.

There are many definitions of entrepreneurship, but one of the earliest and perhaps most relevant to museum entrepreneurship is one developed by economist J.B. Say around 1800: The " entrepreneur shifts economic resources out of an area of lower and into an area of higher productivity and greater yield."[15] In other words, the fundamental question for the museum entrepreneur becomes this: How can we better use our resources to more effectively make ourselves sustainable and relevant?

In their book *Case Studies in Cultural Entrepreneurship*, Gretchen Sorin and Lynne Sessions drill down a bit more and define an *entrepreneur* in the cultural world as a "risk taker who can lead fundamental organizational change through powerful ideas and creative solutions." The authors provide numerous case studies of those organizations in the cultural world that have used entrepreneurial principles to achieve success for their respective institutions.[16] And Brendan Ciecko, founder and CEO of Cuseum, refers to museum entrepreneurs as *"museopreneurs"* and defines them as those "who embrace or assume characteristics of an entrepreneur to advance their museum's business model and general operations."[17]

These definitions can be blended even more for museum purposes by recognizing that most institutions work with limited resources but have unlimited resourcefulness and optimize their resources to make themselves financially and programmatically sustainable. Perhaps a good definition is "the establishment of a culture of innovation and calculated risk-taking that creates sustainable cultural and economic value through use of limited resources."

MUSEUMS AND ENTREPRENEURSHIP

While the pandemic accelerated entrepreneurial activity in museums, entrepreneurship in museums has been around for some time; however, there now exists an increased willingness to recognize that risk-taking, experimentation, and "failing early and failing often" are important components of learning, growing, and finding ways to become sustainable. Museums are also learning the concept of what Drucker calls "organized abandonment"—knowing when programs or experimentation are no longer fruitful and when it is time leave these activities behind and move forward. More than ever, museums are realizing their value in the marketplace by recognizing their unique assets and how they can be monetized and better utilized to benefit both the mission and the bottom line. Examples are plentiful, both large and small.

DEVELOPING FINANCIAL CAPITAL

There is a veritable explosion of museums blending business principles with mission-related goals. An example of this is corporate sponsorships in which museums aggressively promote their unique resources and public standing as leverage to receive corporate support and develop partnerships. The Hammer Museum in Los Angeles, for example, offers sponsorships to businesses noting that "Aligning your brand with an exhibition or program at the Hammer forges awareness of your business with our diverse patrons, supports important cultural initiatives, and provides myriad opportunities for client entertainment and employee engagement."[18]

The Madison Children's Museum in Wisconsin promotes event sponsorships by suggesting businesses participating as sponsors will have opportunities to "connect to wonderfully targeted audiences," and the Whitney Museum of American Art in New York promotes its program as an "opportunity to align your brand with the premiere institution for contemporary American art."[19] In Santa Rosa, California, the Charles M. Schulz Museum promotes sponsorship as "a creative and cost-effective way to engage the public and strengthen your public image while supporting the arts and education," and in Chicago, the National Museum of Mexican Art "offers corporate partners a high level of visibility and close public association with the Museum which is visited by 190,000 visitors annually."[20]

In Kansas City, the National World War I Museum partnered with Waddell & Reed, one of the oldest mutual fund and financial planning companies in the country. The partnership was created out of a desire by the museum to create a national marketing presence and spark interest in the centennial of World War I. Waddell & Reed, in turn, was eager to acknowledge its upcoming seventy-fifth anniversary, engage in national marketing activities, and affiliate itself with the well-known and popular museum. Since the founders of the company were World War I veterans, it was a natural match for the two organizations to join forces. The collaboration resulted in the development of a customized eighteen-wheel "big rig" tractor trailer that was transformed into a traveling World War I exhibition that blended both organizations' interests and honored the upcoming centennial of WWI as well as the institutional history and seventy-fifth anniversary of Waddell & Reed. Promoted as the "Honoring Our History Tour," the project was described as "an ambitious and unconventional acknowledgement" of both anniversaries and traveled to seventy-five cities nationwide.[21]

Ciercko reminds us that " Monetizing internal expertise or other assets, if done in ways that propel a museum's mission, can be tremendously fruitful and beneficial across the board," but "If you do traditional things, you can expect traditional outcomes."[22]

The New Museum in New York created the first museum-led incubator to "support innovation, collaboration, and entrepreneurship across art, design and technology." Called NEW, Inc., the incubator was designed to "foster cultural value, not just capital value" and uses eight thousand square feet of dedicated space as workshops to explore new ways of developing sustainable practices for cultural institutions.[23]

In Massachusetts, Old Sturbridge Village developed its own solar field as a cost-saving measure and established Old Sturbridge Academy, a charter public school that serves a community need while providing a new source of revenue for the Village. The Village also entered into a management agreement to manage the daily operations of Coggeshall Farm Museum, an independent nonprofit organization. Services such as accounting, fundraising, and marketing, for which the Village already has an infrastructure, are provided to Coggeshall Farm for less than the Farm would typically pay for such services. Sturbridge, in turn, receives a new revenue stream, and both organizations benefit.[24]

The Strong National Museum of Play in Rochester, New York, has a long-held commitment to adapting to changing environments and focusing on its strengths. Known for continuous strategic planning and audience research, the museum is currently engaged in a project known as the "Neighborhood of Play." The project is designed to meet both the museum's growing need to provide additional services and the community's need to revitalize the downtown area. Described as the "ultimate destination for all things play," the downtown revitalization project is driven by the Strong's 90,000-square-foot expansion project to enhance exhibitions and create new visitor experiences. The "Neighborhood of Play" will also include a 1,000-car parking garage, rental housing, a mix of retail businesses, and a family-friendly hotel. The new "walkable neighborhood" is expected to attract 400,000 new visitors to the area and generate $130 million in annual economic impact for downtown Rochester.[25]

Museums are also looking inward to monetize their resources. Increasingly common are programs such as that at the Van Gogh Museum in Amsterdam, which promotes a program in which it offers professional museum services to the public and private sector in the areas of conservation, preservation, museum management, and education. The museum estimates that it will allocate as much as 5 to 10 percent of staff time to the initiative and expects the effort to generate as much as 5 percent of total operating revenues. "Museums are used to a different type of outreach that is more about sharing their knowledge and collection, but not in the commercial, contractual manner," said France Desmarais, the director of programs and partnerships for the International Council of Museums in Paris.[26] "It is apt that the museum extends its efforts to include innovative concepts, while naturally endeavoring to strike the correct balance between core museological activities on the one hand, and commercial initiatives on the other," noted managing director Adriaan Dönszelmann.[27]

In Bremen, Germany, the Weserburg Musseum of Modern Art tested a "pay as you stay" admission fee structure in which visitors paid one Euro for every ten minutes spent in the museum. The goal was to create the perception of a fair pricing structure for those visitors with limited time or interest. The program has yielded positive results as both attendance and revenues increased as experimentation with the model continues.[28]

Formerly an industrial complex, MassMoCa (Massachusetts Museum of Contemporary Art) in North Adams, Massachusetts, controls over 550,000 square feet of facilities spread over seventeen buildings.[29] The museum opened in 1999 with little cash and no endowment, but it became successful in large part because it was forced to be "scrappy" and use its lack of resources as a competitive advantage. The founding director, Joseph Thompson, viewed the museum's lack of resources as a "luxury in disguise" as the museum was forced to be resourceful and find ways to successfully blend the commercial with the cultural. The museum has since leased 100,000 square feet of its space for commercial purposes and provides a fee-based artist-in-residency program called The Studios.[30]

The Museum Boijmans van Beuningen in Rotterdam is trying another entrepreneurial approach by renting 10 percent of its new $60 million open-art storage facility to private collectors. Collectors must commit to storing their collection for a minimum of five years at a cost of $400 to $450 per square meter of space. Collections management services are also offered by the museum for an additional fee.[31]

Although not developed directly by a museum, a sound and light show in Toronto of Vincent van Gogh's paintings opened up new possibilities for the museum world. Billed as "Gogh by Car! The World's First Drive-in Immersive Art Exhibit," the fee-based exhibition was set in a former newspaper printing factory and allowed fourteen cars in the space at one time. Visitors were allowed to park inside and enjoy the thirty-five-minute light projections of van Gogh's work along with an original soundtrack. The presentation was developed as a temporary measure in response to social-distancing concerns during the pandemic and designed as a preview to the full five-story exhibition when it was able to safely open to the public.[32]

In Minnesota, the Walker Art Museum in Minneapolis opened its Skyline Mini-Golf course on the museum's rooftop. The ten-hole course was designed by various regional artists. Tickets are $10 for adults, is advertised for all ages, and includes a concession operation. Members, of course, enjoy reduced fees.[33] The John and Mabel Ringling Museum of Art in Florida offered summer "elopement ceremonies" for those whose larger wedding plans were canceled because of social-distancing restrictions. The program was designed for those who "still want the magical, intimate experience of marrying in a beautiful setting." Wedding parties may have a maximum of ten guests, and it costs between $500 and $850, plus a professional photo shoot.[34] And the Evergreen Air and Space Museum in McMinnville, Oregon, home of Howard Hughes's *Spruce Goose*, transformed its parking lot into a camping site for RVs and trailers. A two-night stay was free to campers, but the program was designed to encourage attendance at the museum, which cost $27 per adult.[35]

Many museums responded to the demand for protective masks during the pandemic by producing masks highlighting images from their collections, such as one offered by the Detroit Institute of Arts that highlighted

Diego Rivera's mural *Detroit Industry* from the museum's collections.[36] And the Peabody Essex Museum in Massachusetts offered a wide range of masks featuring images of Chinese porcelain, Japanese kimono prints, and "witches flying over Salem," among many others.[37]

The Curiosity Cruiser is a program offered by the Denver Museum of Nature & Science, in which a pop-up vehicle is "stocked inside and out with fun activities for some on-the-go wonder for all ages." The Curiosity Cruiser is staffed by museum educators who facilitate discovery activities and act as an enhancement at a wide range of community events and locations—"you name it, we'll be there" is the program's tagline. It offers customers a choice of one of three interactive themes—*Flavorology*, *Spicy-Revealed*, and *Mood & Food*—and the cost ranges from $800 to $2,500.[38]

While it is arguably more difficult to generate revenue streams online because so many free resources are available, museums are finding ways to optimize this resource as well. Most virtual courses at the Farnworth Art Museum in Rockland, Maine, give participants an option for payment. The *Field Sketching with Sherrie York* program offers participants a choice of paying the regular fee of $108 or a "Pay what you wish option" because "The Farnsworth understands that these times present economic challenges for many of us. We are committed to making our programming as accessible as possible."[39] The Museum of Science in Boston offers such programs as *STEM AnywhereAnytime* which are designed to help teachers prepare students with "engaging virtual experiences" and prepare them to "implement hands on engineering from a distance." The cost for the program ranges from $179 to $219.[40]

In Kansas City, the National World War I Museum, the Kansas City Actors' Theatre, and the theatre department at the University of Missouri-Kansas City joined forces and blended their resources to create a production of "Oh, What a Lovely War," a 1963 musical satire of World War I. The museum provided the performance space, along with logistical and operational support, while the Actors Theatre provided actors, director, and musical accompaniment. The nineteen-performance event combined the resources of both organizations and successfully achieved the mission-related objectives of the museum, the performance objectives of the Actors' Theatre, and the financial objectives of both organizations. In addition, both organizations introduced their audiences to the respective audiences of the other. The production was a unique collaboration and an overwhelming success. So successful was the program that the two organizations partnered on a second production, "Billy Bishop Goes to War," also a great success.

The Great Lakes Science Center in Cleveland began accepting bitcoin as a means of payment for museum admission. Other early museum bitcoin participants included the St. Petersburg Museum of History in Florida and the Museum of the Coastal Bend in Texas.[41] And online fundraising, which has been around for some time, took on new importance as fundraising programs were built around the pandemic itself.

Such programs as the *Weathering the Storm* campaign developed by Andrew Jackson's Hermitage in Nashville were part of a special funding appeal because "the pandemic has created significant financial challenges" for the Hermitage and funding is essential to ensure continued operation for the "present and future" of the museum.[42] The Paul Revere House in Boston noted on the giving page of its website that its mission had not changed as a result of the pandemic; however, contributions have now become especially important "as we work to recover lost income from our extended closure due to the COVID health emergency."[43] And the Genesee Country Village & Museum in Mumford, New York, noted how their supporters have helped them face "tremendous challenges" during the past year; however, there is "much uncertainty still ahead. And we still need you, now more than ever."[44]

In Las Vegas, the nonprofit Pinball Hall of Fame found itself struggling to complete its expansion during the pandemic and raised $130,000 of a $200,000 goal through a GoFundMe campaign to complete a building project that will house 750 pinball machines.[45]

DEVELOPING CULTURAL CAPITAL

Museums are also being entrepreneurial in using their resources to maintain their relevance and important role in their communities. Often blending creativity, technology, and their unique resources, museums are finding new ways of connecting with their audiences.

In England, the Hastings Contemporary art museum offered free thirty-minute "Robot Tours," which are designed to overcome "barriers of isolation" and create "opportunities to enter the gallery space from the comfort of a sofa, bed, or seat at the kitchen table." The new program also provides easy access to those with disabilities.[46]

The Litchfield Historical Society in Litchfield, Connecticut, noted in its appeal for Annual Fund Giving that the pandemic presented "a much changed environment for us all," but the museum remained "actively engaged with our community in new and exciting ways" with virtual activities for all ages, including a cursive writing course, curatorial talks, and a variety of interactive programs. The development of this effort did not go unnoticed by the museum's constituency. One parent wrote: "The class was definitely a bright spot for Ella, and she looked forward to it every week, which meant a lot as there hasn't been much to look forward to as far as seeing friends or participating in activities."[47]

At the Baltimore Museum of Industry, a planned exhibition on women steel workers ("Women of Steel") was unable to commence because of the tight spaces in the exhibition galleries and the need to provide social distancing. Suddenly "planning an exhibition became an exercise in public health," but the museum adjusted its plans and created the exhibition along a span of fencing on the museum grounds and ultimately opened the exhibition "in a safe open-air environment."[48]

The Chicago History Museum developed its *History at Home Families* program to "support families during these uncertain times," noting that it is "more vital than ever that we stay connected with one another and with our communities." The Museum offers daily programs exploring history, such as *Family History*, in which participants are encouraged to find objects around their homes that reflect family history and then create an exhibition to be shared on social media. Another program is *Oral Histories*, in which family stories are preserved by having younger family members interview older ones. And *Story Time* offers an audio of *Best of the Farm* and then participants make a puppet of their favorite character.[49]

And the Augusta Museum of History announced that it would open the first escape room in the Augusta, Georgia, area, taking place in an actual museum setting in the new exhibit "Augusta 1875–1900."[50] And the Minneapolis Institute of Art opened an escape room app called "Riddle Mia This" that was developed to "unlock a totally new experience of the art."[51]

In Port Townsend, Washington, the Jefferson County Historical Society kept its constituencies engaged through their *Dear 2020* campaign, in which they solicited letters asking "if you were to write a letter from this year, what would it say?" The museum planned to share the letters on social media and in exhibitions and will add them to the museum's collection to create "a lasting record of this historic time."[52]

The Contemporary Arts Museum Houston offered *Virtual Drop-In Experiences*, which were "pop-up" activities that could be done safely at home. The program provided instructions for arts-related creative opportunities to experience museum exhibitions and other programs from a distance. The programs are released every Saturday, and the hands-on activities can be enjoyed anytime. The programs are free and include such things as *Scavenger Hunt for Colors*, in which families are asked to search their homes for objects that reflect the seven colors of the rainbow, noting the variations of similar colors, and then invited make a rainbow of the everyday objects, photograph them, and share them with the museum.[53] *Discovering Art Everywhere* encourages participants to go outdoors, take a walk, and focus on what they see and hear—textures, colors, shapes, sounds—observe things with an artistic eye, and then share their thoughts with each other.

In Karlsruhe, Germany, the Badisches Landesmuseum developed a new app called *My Object*, in which visitors choose from among eighty different objects that interest them. The app then shows them highlights and locations of related exhibits and objects that may interest them. "It's like the dating mobile app Tinder," according to museum director Eckart Koehne. It provides a dialogue with exhibits that interest the visitor.[54]

One can argue that even minor repositioning requires entrepreneurial thought and skill and keeps programs relevant. At the Colonial Williamsburg Foundation, the CDC (no, not the Centers for Disease Control, but rather the Costume Design Center) researchers and tailors worked to ensure that protective masks during the pandemic were as historically accurate as possible, all of which were made on-site of plain fabric. And at Mount Vernon the staff did research on a yellow fever outbreak during George Washington's time and learned that people were advised to wear a handkerchief or scarf to protect themselves from the infectious disease, making it much easier for museum interpreters to enforce mandatory mask-wearing during the pandemic.

International Spy Museum guests are given a "spy gadget" (or stylus) for safe use with the Museum's touchscreens, and pandemic masks were encouraged so guests could visit with spy "disguises." President Abraham Lincoln's Cottage in Washington, DC, advised visitors to "Stay one Lincoln apart from fellow guests" (i.e., 6'4"), and the Witte Museum in San Antonio showed visitors an image of a life-sized bison and encouraged visitors to stay one bison apart from each other and then, in an attempt to add a new line of revenue-producing merchandise, offered an image of that same bison on T-shirts sold in the museum store.[55]

The Virginia Museum of Fine Arts offers *VMFA on the Road: An Artmobile for the 21st Century*, which is a temperature- and humidity-controlled fifty-three-foot state-of-the-art tractor trailer. Initiated in 2018, the program was designed to provide "the opportunity for residents of the Commonwealth to see and experience works of art from the VMFA collections up close." Although artmobiles are nothing new, this particular program was designed to travel specifically to remote areas of Virginia, and admission is free.[56]

THE COURAGE TO CHANGE

Change is difficult. It can be disruptive, almost always creates a sense of uncertainty, and frequently results in a default response of resistance–sometimes even hostility. Change is often resisted even when traditional practices are no longer working. Breaking out of an entrenched "we've always done it that way" culture is challenging when an organization has been accustomed to the safety and comfort of predictability in the workplace. Yet the very nature of entrepreneurship and leadership is about change and movement. There must be a willingness to change and adapt, but therein rests the major challenge. Change is not always easy. Jerr Boshee notes that "the embedded culture of an organization so often (is) the single greatest obstacle" to innovation and entrepreneurship.[57]

Change by its very nature requires experimentation and risk-taking, both of which can be unsettling. Change is resisted because it is unfamiliar, but resistance also prevents forward movement. Change may not always produce the desired result, but not changing guarantees paralysis. Much can be learned from setbacks if things do not work as planned. But we must *do* something. Nothing gets better unless there is a willingness to change. Again, to quote Brendan Ciercko, "If you do traditional things, you can expect traditional outcomes."[58]

Making major institutional change is complicated, requires careful thought, and takes great courage and determination. Perhaps the most well-known change-management approach is that created by John P. Kotter. Entitled "The 8-Step Process for Leading Change," the Kotter program was based on over four decades of research and observation of companies instituting change. Kotter articulated a systematic, step-by-step approach beginning with creating a sense of urgency and providing a clear reason for the change to how change is effected, sustained, and incorporated into the institutional culture.[59]

An example of courage and determination to implement change was the transformation of the Indianapolis Museum of Art when it determined to fundamentally change the nature of the museum experience. Museum leaders recognized the need for the museum to broaden its appeal to its audiences and increase revenues, and consequently made controversial changes in its operation. In 2017 the museum united all of its "unique assets" on its 152-acre campus—including museum galleries, gardens, the historic Lilly House, and an Art & Nature Park with one hundred acres, a thirty-five-acre lake, walking trails, and various performance spaces.

The goal of the new approach was to provide "exceptional experiences with art and nature" to be "enjoyed by guests of all ages, interest areas, and backgrounds." It was believed that the experiences could be "life changing, or they might be good just for a laugh." The "unique assets" would come together as one entity and be rebranded under a new name: "Newfields, a Place for Nature and the Arts."[60]

Newfields' new emphasis was to provide visitors, from families to sophisticated art lovers, with a full menu of optional experiences, with the ultimate goal of serving more people and growing revenue. The museum introduced such initiatives as a craft beer garden on the museum's grounds, a pop-up mini-golf course, a pumpkin show, a cat-video festival, and a tea house, among others. One of the most successful programs was the "Winterlight Festival," for which visitors paid $25 to view over one million holiday lights placed around the grounds while *The Nutcracker Suite* played in the background.

Not everyone was happy with the changes. Critics accused the museum of "dumbing down" the museum, but it was clear that if the museum was to remain relevant and sustainable, it had to change. There were clashes with members of the public and peers in the museum field (including the museum's own employees) who were entrenched in the traditions of what the museum had always been. One museum director expressed concern that the Newfields' approach would "lose the reason we have museums in the first place—as a wonderful oasis, not a midwestern boardwalk." They felt that the new direction had become "a travesty."[61]

Although still eager for visitors to enjoy the museum's vast art collections, the museum's position was that not everyone had an interest in art. As a result, the Newfields' experience would no longer be one-dimensional because it would now appeal to many ages and interests. Thanks to the museum's commitment to change, earned income increased, debt was reduced by $40 million, the amount of income drawn from the endowment decreased, and the board began planning a capital campaign.[62] "I think if the art museum industry does not follow the lead of other industries, there is a looming crisis in which galleries full of the world's truly greatest creative art will be empty. And that is not going to happen here," said the museum's director.[63]

While the evidence of successful change was impressive by every metric, problems later arose for Newfields when a job advertisement suggested Newfields' ongoing goal was broadening visitorship while maintaining its core "white" audiences. It remains to be seen how this misstep will affect Newfields' progress.

SOME KEY CONCEPTS

There are a number of concepts for museum entrepreneurs to think about as they embrace change to help ensure programmatic and financial sustainability. Here is a list of some things to consider:

UNFAIR ADVANTAGES

Every organization has unfair advantages. Unfair advantages are those resources that your organization possesses that cannot be easily copied, or do not wish to be copied, by competitors. Unfair advantages may be staff expertise or institutional networks. They may be unique or extensive collections or a campus-like setting such as that at Newfields. Adaptable indoor spaces such as those at Mass MoCa, or special affiliations or relationships such as that of Old Sturbridge Village with filmmaker Ken Burns, may all be considered unfair advantages.

Unfair advantages may also be an enthusiastic, hardworking, or influential board of trustees; special endorsements such as Kevin Costner's pro bono commercials for the National World War I Museum; a large museum membership or customer base or just leadership that embraces change to create a culture of experimentation. It can be practically anything. Every organization is blessed with at least some if not multiple advantages. It is about identifying these advantages and utilizing them to create value and uniquely position an organization in the marketplace.

LACK OF RESOURCES . . . OR RESOURCEFULNESS?

One of the common concerns in the museum field is that there is a lack of operational funding and dreams of exploring new initiatives seem like a financial impossibility. Certainly funding is a chronic problem, and more funding would be ideal, but lack of funding can also be used as an excuse to move forward. There may be limits on financial resources, but resourcefulness is limited only by one's imagination and willingness to experiment and work hard. Daymond John suggests that it is about "tapping into the mindset that finds us . . . when we are in "that place of desperation" and "putting it to work *for* you instead of *against* you."[64] John even goes so far as to say that having a plentiful supply of money can actually be a disadvantage because when there is a lack of money, we must "work harder, smarter, faster, longer," which ultimately creates "a kind of competitive edge."[65]

EFFECTUAL REASONING

In a study entitled "What Makes Entrepreneurs Entrepreneurial?" University of Virginia Professor Saras Sarasvathy writes that entrepreneurs, especially in the early stages of entrepreneurial activity, tend not to be causal thinkers—i.e., thinkers who begin with a certain set of specific goals in mind and predetermined resources to achieve their goals. The essence of causal thinking is that the future can be predicted. Instead, entrepreneurs tend to be effectual thinkers.

Effectual thinking is especially useful and productive for entrepreneurs in solving problems. It does not begin with a specific goal in mind; instead it "begins with a given set of means and allows goals to emerge contingently over time from the varied imagination and diverse aspirations" of those leading the charge and those they learn from—i.e., they assess available resources and then allow goals to emerge organically. Effectual thinkers make connections with available, known resources to make ideas come to life.

Sarasvathy suggests that causal thinkers are akin to explorers, or "great generals seeking to conquer fertile lands (Genghis Khan conquering two-thirds of the known world), as opposed to effectual thinkers, who are "like explorers setting out on voyages into uncharted waters (Columbus discovering the New World)." Putting it into more modern terms, causal thinkers are like chefs who select a recipe and then proceed to obtain the ingredients to make the best meal possible, but effectual thinkers are like contestants on the reality television show *Chopped*, who work with an already available set of ingredients to create the best meal possible.[66]

Utilizing resources that already exist is a realistic, achievable, and affordable way to move forward, but it requires resourcefulness and an understanding of a museum's unfair advantages.

CREATIVE IMITATION

Creative imitation means that an organization or business imitates something that already exists, but it adds a new value or distinguishing feature that others do not have. In many cases, the "imitation" builds upon the successes of the original, but reduces or eliminates its mistakes and adds a dimension that fills a need in the marketplace. It is simply changed or adapted to meet the needs of consumers. Creative imitation is about improving an existing product or service and creating characteristics that others have not thought of or do not wish to pursue. It is a value-added enhancement of what already exists.[67]

Classic examples of creative imitation exist all around us. FedEx, UPS, and others built upon already-existing package delivery services from the United States Postal Service and began to offer next-day and even same-day delivery services. Amazon built upon online shopping platforms and revolutionized the industry by creating comprehensive shopping and delivery services. Xerox dominated the office copier industry in the 1950s and 1960s but focused more on larger users—new manufacturers in Japan soon swooped in to build smaller copiers and appeal to smaller organizations. Carvana built upon online shopping for automobiles by essentially eliminating dealerships and even delivering cars to consumers as early as the next day. These companies did not invent package delivery, copiers, or online shopping. Instead they knew their competitors well, learned from them, and added value to already-existing products or services. Not being the first to introduce new services has advantages by allowing us to learn from others' omissions or mistakes. Let others do the heavy lifting.

FINDING AN "EMPTY PLACE" AND CREATING VALUE

In the business world, nine of ten entrepreneurial startups fail, often because they create a product or service that no one wants and little or no value has been created around the product or service.[68] Brilliant inventions are not uncommon, but ultimately they only matter if there is value built around them. They must serve an existing need, or a perceived value must be created. Otherwise, a new program may be clever, but it quickly dies because no one cares. Drucker notes that many inventors have developed as many as forty or more inventions, but they failed in the marketplace because there was no perceived need for them. Creating things that no one wants is futile work.

This, of course, underscores the need for a thorough understanding of customer needs, desires, and interests. As organizations experiment with and refine new programs, it is not just about ironing out program logistics and presentation. The *value* of the product or service must be evaluated carefully. Does it matter to the consumer? If so, how and why? Finding that value may take some creativity and the ability to connect some dots, but staying close to the customer is critical. Former editor-in-chief of *Business Week* Lew Young noted that "Probably the most important management fundamental that is being ignored today is staying close to the customer to satisfy his needs and anticipate his wants."[69] Nothing matters if the customer is not interested.

"READY, FIRE, AIM"

Nearly forty years ago, Thomas J. Peters and Robert H. Waterman Jr. attributed this quote to an executive at Cadbury, the British confectionery company. Peters and Waterman emphasized that planning sometimes becomes an end unto itself rather than a means to achieve certain ends. They wrote that truly successful companies have "an action orientation, a bias for getting things done," and they "try things out, to experiment."[70] Waiting for every question to be answered and analyzing things ad infinitum becomes an excuse for doing, and more can be gained from testing, prototyping, and getting ideas into the hands of customers as soon as possible. Entrepreneurs research, test, refine, and learn by anticipating certain levels of failure as necessary to create an effective product. This approach, also known as design thinking, consists of five basic steps: 1) *Empathize* by understanding the customer's needs and desires, 2) *Define* the problem based on research and understanding of the customer, 3) *Ideate* possible solutions through creative brainstorming, 4) *Prototype* and consult with the customer to learn more as the basics are presented and then refine accordingly, and 5) *Test* or launch the project to see if it works, or provides additional insights for continued improvement.[71]

Entrepreneurs expect to fail at times, but they know that much is learned from failure. "Fail early, fail often" is the entrepreneurial mantra, and successful entrepreneurship may take many attempts, but each time something is learned and the project is made better.

CALCULATED RISK TAKING

Making change implies a certain level of risk because the fully tested and proven initiatives from the past are being left behind in favor of new, untested directions. And taking risks when there are volunteers, staff, trustees, community leaders, funders, and other stakeholders involved makes change infinitely more daunting. Yet if there is a unwillingness to take risks, there can be no benefit from the potential returns of taking that risk. In other words, not taking risks means that there is little likelihood of productive change.

Museums take risks every day, but they are so ingrained in the museum work culture that they are seldom thought of as risks. Outdoor museums run the risk of inclement weather, which may have a devastating impact on attendance. The security of collections is at risk when objects are exhibited in galleries. Revenue streams are at risk at every turn because most museum revenues are not guaranteed and rely on market conditions. The success of public programming is at risk when new programs are offered. There is a risk in selecting trustees and staff. Everything has an element of risk, but that risk can be minimized with sound preparation that attempts to weigh the level of risk against the likely return or benefit. The trick is to take chances that are well-considered and thoughtful. Growth is not possible without some level of risk, and if organizations are risk-averse, the likelihood of growth and productive change is unlikely.

Researcher Sally Caird calls this "calculated risk taking" and defines it as "the ability to deal with incomplete information and act on a risky option"; it "requires skill to actualize challenging but realistic goals." Author and business consultant Larry Alton provides six simple steps for calculated risk-taking that are applicable for museums and are summarized as follows: 1) *Conduct Due Diligence & Research*—Understand and analyze decisions and base them on good information; 2) *Anticipate Mistakes*—Think about positive and negative outcomes and how they will be handled; 3) *Establish Checkpoints*—Develop short-term goals to stay on track for the overall goal; 4) *Be Ready to Pivot*—Anticipate organizational response if circumstances change; 5) *Learn to Say No*—Stay committed to those initiatives that have the best chance of succeeding; and 6) *Take Action When the Moment Is Right*—Trust research and judgment and take the leap.[72]

"ORGANIZED ABANDONMENT"

Museums cannot do everything. As they become more entrepreneurial and experiment with new directions, they must also recognize that to move forward, not all baggage (good or bad) can be carried into the future. Sometimes it becomes necessary to release resources that are committed to projects that are no longer or are not likely to be productive. Ultimately concern must be focused on results and effectiveness, not the maintenance of those things that have become entrenched in the institutional culture. Such things become burdensome, are time-consuming, and cost money and staff time. Resources might be better used for more productive initiatives. There must be an organized process to judge when a project is no longer viable, because if museums are unwilling to change, they cannot move forward. Drucker notes that if an organization's resources are "committed to maintaining yesterday, they are simply not available to create tomorrow."[73]

SUMMARY

The examples of museum entrepreneurship in this chapter are a few of many that have key characteristics in common. Museums found many ways to maximize their resources, use their competitive advantages, and create value. And they had the courage to change.

ORGANIZATIONS THAT ENJOY SUCCESS:

Embrace change as a natural part of institutional growth.

Cultivate and encourage an ongoing culture of experimentation, take calculated risks, and learn from mistakes.

Stay close to the customer and always look for opportunities to add value and effectively use resources.

Recognize their unique assets and "unfair advantages."

Think boldly and proceed methodically and judiciously, but do not "overplan."

Learn from others and build upon existing ideas.

Work hard to refine and develop projects, but also know when to abandon them.

NOTES

1. "United States May Lose One-Third of All Museums, New Survey Shows," American Alliance of Museums, July 22, 2020, https://www.aam-us.org/2020/07/22/united-states-may-lose-one-third-of-all-museums-new-survey-shows/.
2. "About Peter Drucker," Drucker Institute, accessed January 15, 2021, https://www.drucker.institute/perspective/about-peter-drucker/.
3. Peter Drucker, *Innovation and Entrepreneurship: Practice and Principles* (Oxford, U.K.: Butterworth-Heinemann, 1985), 177.

4. Ibid., 178; see also ibid., 28.
5. Lonnie Bunch, "A Vision for Museums: A Conversation with the Secretary of the Smithsonian," Lecture, Cooperstown Graduate Program, Cooperstown, NY, October 30, 2020.
6. Daymond John and Daniel Paisner, *The Power of Broke: How Empty Pockets, a Tight Budget, and a Hunger for Success Can Become Your Greatest Competitive Advantage* (New York, NY: Crown Business, 2016), 10–11.
7. J. Gregory Dees, Jed Emerson, and Peter Economy, *Enterprising Nonprofits: A Toolkit for Social Entrepreneurs* (New York, NY: John Wiley and Sons, 2001), 1.
8. "Museum Facts and Data," American Alliance of Museums, accessed January 17, 2020, https://www.aam-us.org/programs/about-museums/museum-facts-data/.
9. Boschee, "Smart Nonprofit Leaders Are Finding Opportunity in Scarcity."
10. Drucker, *Innovation and Entrepreneurship: Practice and Principles*, 139.
11. Ibid., 133.
12. Thomas J. Peters and Robert H. Waterman Jr., *In Search of Excellence: Lessons from America's Best-Run Companies* (New York, NY: HarperCollins, 1983), 170.
13. John and Paisner, *The Power of Broke: How Empty Pockets, a Tight Budget, and a Hunger for Success Can Become Your Greatest Competitive Advantage*, 31.
14. Peters and Waterman, *In Search of Excellence: Lessons from America's Best-Run Companies*, 119.
15. Drucker, *Innovation and Entrepreneurship: Practice and Principles*, 21.
16. Gretchen Sullivan Sorin and Lynne A. Sessions, *Case Studies in Cultural Entrepreneurship: How to Create Relevant and Sustainable Institutions* (Lanham, MD: Rowman & Littlefield, 2015), ix.
17. Brendan Ciecko, "Museopreneur: How Museums Are Leaping into New Business Models with Entrepreneurial Spirit," American Alliance of Museums, May 3, 2019, https://www.aam-us.org/2019/05/03/museopreneur-how-museums-are-leap ing-into-new-business-models-with-entrepreneurial-spirit/.
18. "Corporate Sponsorships," Hammer Museum, accessed January 17, 2021, https://hammer.ucla.edu/support/sponsorship-opportunities.
19. "For Companies," Madison Children's Museum, accessed January 17, 2021, https://madisonchildrensmuseum.org/support/corporate-giving/; see also "Corporate Sponsorships," Whitney Museum of American Art, accessed January 17, 2021, https://whitney.org/Support/Corporate/Sponsorship.
20. "Corporate Sponsorship," Charles M. Schulz Museum, accessed January 17, 2021, https://schulzmuseum.org/get-involved/corporate-support/coporate-sponsorship/; see also "Corporate Sponsorship," National Museum of Mexican Art, accessed January 17, 2021, https://nationalmuseumofmexicanart.org/content/corporate-sponsorship.
21. "Waddell & Reed's Traveling World War I Exhibition," Lyon Air Museum, accessed January 17, 2021, https://lyonairmuseum.org/blog/waddell-reeds-travel ing-world-war-i-exhibition/.
22. Ciecko, "Museopreneur: How Museums Are Leaping into New Business Models with Entrepreneurial Spirit."
23. "NEW INC," New Museum, accessed January 17, 2021, https://www.newmuseum .org/pages/view/new-inc-1#:~:text=NEW%20INC%20is%20a%20creative%20 ecosystem%20that%20aims,to%20foster%20cultural%20value%2C%20not%20 just%20capital%20value.

24. Jim Donahue, "Announcing a New Historic Partnership in 2020," Old Sturbridge Village, accessed January 17, 2021, https://www.osv.org/content/uploads/2019/12/Letter-from-Jim-Donahue1.pdf.
25. "Expansion Project," The Strong Museum of Play, accessed January 17, 2021, http://www.museumofplay.org/expansion-campaign/expansion-project.
26. Nina Siegal, "Van Gogh Museum Wants to Share Its Expertise, for a Price," *New York Times* (New York, NY), May 4, 2016, https://www.nytimes.com/2016/05/04/arts/design/van-gogh-museum-wants-to-share-its-expertise-for-a-price.html.
27. Ciecko, "Museopreneur: How Museums Are Leaping into New Business Models with Entrepreneurial Spirit."
28. Elizabeth Merritt, "'Pay As You Stay'—an alternative pricing model for museums?," American Alliance of Museums, July 15, 2020, https://www.aam-us.org/2020/07/15/pay-as-you-stay-an-alternative-pricing-model-for-museums/.
29. Colin Moynihan, "MASS MoCA's Founding Director to Step Down," *New York Times*, August 21, 2020, https://www.nytimes.com/2020/08/21/arts/design/mass-moca-director-to-step-down.html.
30. Ciecko, "Museopreneur: How Museums Are Leaping into New Business Models with Entrepreneurial Spirit."
31. "Rotterdam Museum Will Begin Renting Public Space to Private Collectors," Art Forum, February 10, 2016, https://www.artforum.com/news/rotterdam-museum-will-begin-renting-public-space-to-private-collectors-58054.
32. Naomi Rea, "Van Gogh at the Drive-Thru? As Museums Remain on Lockdown, a Toronto Exhibition Is Treating Viewers to the Dutch Master's Art in Their Cars," ArtNet News, May 18, 2020, https://news.artnet.com/art-world/drive-in-van-gogh-1863576.
33. "Skyline Mini Golf 2019," Walker Art Center, accessed January 17, 2021, https://walkerart.org/calendar/2019/skyline-mini-golf-2019.
34. Allison Forsyth, "Ringling Museum Offering Special Elopement Ceremonies to Couples," *Sarasota Magazine*, July 9, 2020, https://www.sarasotamagazine.com/fashion-and-shopping/2020/07/ringling-museum-offering-special-elopement-ceremonies-to-couples.
35. "Evergreen Air and Space Museum," Free Campsites, accessed January 18, 2021, https://freecampsites.net/#!88219&query=sitedetails.
36. "Detroit Industry South Wall, Rivera Face Mask," Detroit Institute of Arts, accessed January 18, 2021, https://diashop.org/detroit-industry-south-wall-rivera-face-mask/.
37. "Masks," Peabody Essex Museum, accessed January 18, 2021, https://pemshop.com/collections/masks.
38. "Curiosity Cruiser," Denver Museum of Nature and Science, accessed January 18, 2021, https://www.dmns.org/visit/in-the-community/curiosity-cruiser/.
39. "Field Sketching with Sherrie York," Farnsworth Art Museum, accessed January 18, 2021, https://www.farnsworthmuseum.org/event/field-sketching-with-sherrie-york-2020-07-01-2/.
40. "Engineering Is Elementary," Museum of Science, Boston, accessed January 18, 2021, https://www.eventbrite.com/o/eie-museum-of-science-boston-8004233151.
41. Jeremy Nobile, "Great Lakes Science Center: We Take Bitcoin," Crain's Cleveland Business, November 9, 2018, https://www.crainscleveland.com/arts-entertainment/great-lakes-science-center-we-take-bitcoin.

42. "Your Support Is Essential," Andrew Jackson's Hermitage, accessed January 18, 2021, https://thehermitage.com/donate-today/.
43. "Why Give?," Paul Revere House, accessed January 18, 2021, https://www.paul reverehouse.org/why-give/.
44. "Give Now," Genesee Country Village and Museum, accessed January 18, 2021, https://www.gcv.org/give-join/give-now/.
45. Kate Silver, "Could GoFundMe campaigns save our cultural collections? Las Vegas's Pinball Hall of Fame is banking on it," *Washington Post*, February 26, 2021, https://www.washingtonpost.com/lifestyle/travel/pinball-hall-of-fame-las-ve gas/2021/02/25/0295bac4-6c80-11eb-ba56-d7e2c8defa31_story.html.
46. "Robot Tours," Hastings Contemporary, accessed January 18, 2021, https://www .hastingscontemporary.org/exhibition/robot-tours/.
47. "Annual Fund," Litchfield Historical Society, accessed January 18, 2021, https://www .litchfieldhistoricalsociety.org/annual-fund/.
48. Beth Maloney and Claire Mullins, "Curating During a Pandemic: A Lesson in Democracy and Fresh Air," American Association for State and Local History, November 16, 2020, https://aaslh.org/curating-during-a-pandemic/.
49. "Chicago History at Home Families," Chicago History Museum, accessed January 18, 2021, https://www.chicagohistory.org/chicago-history-at-home-families/.
50. "Museum Escape: Murder at the Mill," Augusta Museum of History, accessed January 18, 2021, https://www.augustamuseum.org/MurderAtTheMill.
51. Gretchen Halverson, "Introducing "Riddle Mia This, The Museum's New Escape-Room App," Minneapolis Institute of Art, August 29, 2018, https://medium.com/minneap olis-institute-of-art/introducing-riddle-mia-this-the-museums-new-escape-room -app-65c8c6e907d9.
52. "Dear 2020," Jefferson County Historical Society, accessed January 18, 2021, https:// www.jchsmuseum.org/GetInvolved/Dear-2020.html.
53. "Scavenger Hunt for Colors | Virtual Drop-In Experience," Contemporary Arts Museum Houston, accessed January 18, 2021, https://camh.org/event/scaven ger-hunt-colors-virtual-drop-experience/.
54. German Press Agency, "German museum's new app matches visitors to artifacts," *Daily Sabah* (Istanbul, Turkey), February 16, 2021, https://www.dailysabah.com/arts /german-museums-new-app-matches-visitors-to-artifacts/news?utm _source=American+Alliance+of+Museums&utm_campaign=5353b6ef36-DIS PATCHES_February25_2021&utm_medium=email&utm_term=0_f06e575db6 -5353b6ef36-37342473.
55. Vicky Hallett, "At Tourist Sites, Masking Up Without Diluting The Experience," *Washington Post* (Washington, DC), November 23, 2020, https://www .washingtonpost.com/lifestyle/travel/safety-precautions-williamsburg-disney-ve gas/2020/11/23/2bd7a90c-281e-11eb-8fa2-06e7cbb145c0_story.html.
56. "VMFA on the Road," Virginia Museum of Fine Arts, accessed January 18, 2021, https://www.vmfa.museum/exhibitions/exhibitions/vmfa-on-the-road/.
57. Jerr Boschee, "Smart Nonprofit Leaders are Finding Opportunity in Scarcity," Cause Planet, accessed January 18, 2021, http://socialent.org/documents/THESINGLE GREATESTCHALLENGE.pdf.
58. Ciecko, "Museopreneur: How Museums are Leaping into New Business Models with Entrepreneurial Spirit."

59. "The 8-Step Process for Leading Change," Kotter, Inc., accessed January 18, 2021, https://www.kotterinc.com/8-steps-process-for-leading-change/.
60. "Director's Welcome," Newfields, a Place for Nature and the Arts.
61. Alina Tugend, "To Reach New Audiences, Museums Are Redefining What They Offer," *New York Times*, March 12, 2018, https://www.nytimes.com/2018/03/12/arts/to-reach-new-audiences-museums-are-redefining-what-they-offer.html.
62. Andrew Russeth, "The Ringmaster: Is Charles Venable Democratizing a Great Art Museum in Indianapolis—or Destroying it?"
63. Tugend, "To Reach New Audiences, Museums Are Redefining What They Offer."
64. John and Paisner, *The Power of Broke: How Empty Pockets, a Tight Budget, and a Hunger for Success Can Become Your Greatest Competitive Advantage*, 39.
65. John and Paisner, *The Power of Broke: How Empty Pockets, a Tight Budget, and a Hunger for Success Can Become Your Greatest Competitive Advantage*, 31.
66. "What Makes Entrs Entl," Society for Effectual Action, accessed January 18, 2021, https://www.effectuation.org/.
67. Peter Drucker, "Driving Business Growth Through the Practice of Creative Imitation: Part II," Management Matters Network, accessed January 18, 2021, https://www.managementmattersnetwork.com/innovation-entrepreneurship/articles/driving-business-growth-through-the-practice-of.
68. Neil Patel, "90% of Startups Will Fail. Here's What You Need to Know About the 10%," *Forbes*, January 16, 2015, https://www.forbes.com/sites/neilpatel/2015/01/16/90-of-startups-will-fail-heres-what-you-need-to-know-about-the-10/?sh=1c6b69656679.
69. Peters and Waterman, *In Search of Excellence: Lessons from America's Best-Run Companies*, 156.
70. Ibid., 119; see also ibid., 134.
71. "Design Thinking Process," GP Strategies, accessed January 18, 2021, https://www.gpstrategies.com/design-thinking-process/.
72. Larry Alton, "How Entrepreneurs Can Take Calculated Risks," *Small Business Trends*, April 3, 2016, https://smallbiztrends.com/2016/04/entrepreneurs-taking-calculated-risks.html#:~:text=%206%20Tips%20for%20Taking%20Calculated%20Risks%20,may%20be%20months%20or%20years%20away.%20More%20.
73. "Leadership Notes on Peter Drucker on Organized Abandonment," Rutherford Learning Group, accessed January 18, 2021, https://rutherfordlg.com/rlg_new/wp-content/uploads/2016/08/Leadership-Notes-Peter-Drucker-on-Organized-Abandonment120517-1.pdf.

4

Diversifying with Care

The search for predictable revenue streams is part of daily life in every museum. Independent nonprofit museums conduct a range of revenue-producing activities depending on their needs and resources. Different museums focus on different things, but revenue streams generally fall into four major categories: Government Support (tax-based and grant funding), Earned Income (fees for goods or services), Unearned Income (private donations), and Investment Income (primarily endowment). Within each major category, there are many specific initiatives. Individual contributions, corporate and foundation gifts, and bequests are among unearned income activities. Retail sales, food service operations, facility rentals, admissions, and program fees are typical of earned income. Investment income is primarily from endowment but may include earnings from other short- and long-term investments.[1]

Many museums diversify as much as possible to spread out revenue sources in the event that one area suffers a significant downturn. They prefer not to "put all their eggs in one basket." Others diversify, but with a particular emphasis on certain streams related to their unique assets or those that have traditionally brought great success. Still others diversify very little, rely on too few revenue streams, and hope that these remain strong into the future. Each museum distributes or focuses its financial "eggs" differently.

Museums depend on certain revenue sources in varying degrees. Institutions with large endowments are more inclined to lean more heavily on endowment because they have the resources to do so. Some organizations may have good attendance, but a relatively small endowment and focus more on gate-related earned income. Still others suffer from low attendance and no endowment and usually focus more on the generosity of donors. Much depends on the circumstances of each museum.

Every revenue stream has degrees of predictability. Some sources are highly volatile while others remain relatively stable from year to year. Other areas have potential to earn high revenues, but are subject to higher risk. Still others are less risky, but show relatively little growth. Endowment income, for example, is usually relatively stable if investments are mixed in terms of risk level and return, but the endowment is still dependent on the stock market. And even when there are gains in the market, endowment income draw is unlikely to show dramatic income growth because it takes an enormous amount of funds in endowment principal to generate significant operational income. Unearned income is dependent on the economy and donors' inclination to give and can fluctuate wildly from year to year. Earned income is dependent on a competitive marketplace, the appeal of museum programs and services, and even the weather. There are plenty of risks to go around—and many are often beyond the control of the museum.

Every museum would like funding sources to be assured and grow for the long term, but often they do not. Bad things happen. Funding interests of donors change, the state of the economy changes, donor funds are depleted, government priorities change, a museum's new direction may no longer be compatible with the funder, or funders may simply want to distribute contributions in other areas. Many other complications exist that throw revenue streams into turmoil; for example, stretches of inclement weather are often devastating or visitors may tire of a museum if it does not maintain a relevant and dynamic program. Sometimes major calamities present themselves, such as the recession of 2008 or the extraordinary impact of COVID-19. The pandemic in particular had a profound impact on museum financial stability and created a crisis in the field.

OVER-RELIANCE ON TOO FEW SOURCES

Sometimes major funding generated from one or two sources creates a false sense of financial security. Perhaps the museum has relied heavily on a few sources of revenue for years. Generous donors are always there, earned income grows steadily, and a good stock market propels growth in the endowment. It is easy to think that such funding will continue for years to come. Focusing on the likelihood of losing a long-standing major revenue stream simply is not a priority because losing that revenue stream does not seem likely—until the day it is lost. Then an existential crisis presents itself. One major art museum in Los Angeles, for example, relied on donors for 80 percent of its funding, but found itself in serious trouble during the financial crisis of 2008, when its unearned revenue was significantly diminished.[2]

When one or two major revenue sources carry the weight of financial support and these sources suddenly disappear or are drastically reduced, the museum finds itself facing a major threat to its survival. The institution is forced to find significant replacement funding quickly and often without obvious sources to call upon. The usual viable options are to borrow money to stay afloat; borrow internally from an endowment or other sources if available; make an emergency funding appeal; close temporarily; or, as a last resort, close permanently. Borrowing from the endowment is dangerous because it is often not repaid, and thus ultimately impacts the endowment's ability to generate income in the future. Certainly, a generous donor can swoop in to make a major gift to eradicate the crisis, but this type of support is likely to be one-time. This was the experience of the Castlemaine Art Museum in Australia, when a last-minute gift of $250,000 by private donors saved the museum—at least temporarily.[3] This was a short-term solution that probably could not be relied upon in subsequent years. In still other cases, especially during the desperate times of the pandemic crisis, museums looked increasingly to the controversial use of deaccessioning sale proceeds as a last resort to support ongoing operational needs.[4]

One history museum in a major metropolitan area lost its primary funding from the city in which it was located and closed in 2018 after it struggled for years to broaden its base of sustainable funding. Beginning in the 1990s, the museum sought to find "long-term financial viability" through such efforts as rebranding; a major renovation of its historic building; new programming; expanded fund-raising efforts; introduction of admission fees; and a search for viable, sustainable partnerships with other museums and local universities.[5] Unfortunately, the loss of major city funding received "in a significant way, for years" proved too much for the museum.[6] Without major support from the city, the museum was forced to close its doors permanently.[7]

The New Jersey Museum of Agriculture Museum, founded in 1984 on the campus of Rutgers University, struggled for survival when its entire state-funded appropriation was eliminated. The museum always had its share of financial difficulties, but such a reduction was more than the museum could handle. It sought new funding sources to replace the lost revenue, but faced the very real possibility of auctioning off the collections and closing permanently.[8] The delegates of the New Jersey Agricultural Convention repeatedly called upon "all New Jersey agricultural organizations" for support as well as for the "Governor and the Legislature to continue to support the New Jersey Museum of Agriculture by identifying a stable funding source for Museum operations and restoring a funding level of at least $180,000 per year."[9] Despite its best efforts and a school program that served as many as 123 schools and 9,724 students in 2004 alone, the loss of this single source of funding forced the museum to close its doors in 2011.[10]

Many governmental institutions face special challenges as they are often prohibited from directly soliciting private funding. When significant government reductions are instituted, these museums are forced to adapt to the reductions unless they have a support organization designed to raise money for specific purposes for the museum. Typical of such support organizations is the State Historical Society of North Dakota Foundation, which is a "private, non-profit organization supported by membership and donations." The Foundation was formed to "generate private financial support for the State Historical Society's projects and programs that cannot be funded by the legislature."[11] Major operational reductions, however, are unlikely to be made up regardless of whether there is a supporting organization to raise funds on behalf of the museum because funding needs are so great.

Reliant largely on state funding, the Illinois State Museum was threatened with closure in 2015, when the governor's budget proposal recommended elimination of the entire $6.9 million funding allocation for the museum. The chair of the museum board noted that the governor's cuts would be "devastating to the museum," and the American Alliance of Museums noted that closure would likely result in the museum's accreditation being revoked because it would no longer have "enough financial resources . . . to be a sustainable, viable organization." While the museum received various other forms of operating support, the shortfall of $6.9 million was impossible to make up, and the museum was forced to close temporarily.[12]

Perhaps the most dramatic and striking example of over-reliance on one revenue source was that of the Newseum in Washington, DC. The Newseum was heavily reliant on the Freedom Forum for funding, but when it became evident that the Freedom Forum could no longer support the museum at high levels, the Newseum had no choice but to cease operations in its new facility. Ultimately the property was put on the market and eventually purchased by Johns Hopkins University for $372.5 million.[13]

Many museums have recognized that relying on too few revenue streams makes them extremely vulnerable when those sources are diminished or no longer forthcoming. Often there is no warning, and museums suddenly face an unexpected, existential crisis that threatens the very viability of the museum.

Located in East Meredith, New York, Hanford Mills Museum is a seventy-acre site that includes sixteen historic structures and an operating sawmill. The museum is a well-run institution but faces challenges typical of rural museums. While offering a range of programs to engage audiences, the museum attracts a relatively modest audience because of its location. Earned and unearned financial support are limited—except for one foundation that provides well over one-half of the museum's unrestricted operating support.[14] The prospect of losing that single revenue source would create an existential threat to the museum. Trustees responded by including in their strategic plan the goal to "develop diversified and sustainable revenue sources to ensure ongoing operations."[15]

The Sherman Museum in Sherman, Texas, saw its budget allocation reduced significantly by the Sherman city council in 2019. The city council used the budget reduction as a way to force the museum to diversify its funding base as a condition for the city to provide additional funds. The council stipulated that the museum would be eligible to receive additional funds only if it found funding matches outside city funding. The funding challenge was designed to encourage the museum to look for more community support and grants and not rely so much on the city. "It has been a priority of the city for about five years now to push the museum to seek funds from other sources than the city coffers," according to one city official. The city, which resisted reducing museum funding for years, determined that it could no longer support the museum at previous levels because of other demands on city funds. The new strategy came at a difficult time for the museum as it struggled with significant and expensive repairs to its two buildings, but it has continued to operate.[16]

In Amarillo, Texas, the Panhandle-Plains Historical Museum state budget in 2019 was reduced by 30 percent with another 30 percent reduction planned for the following year. As a result, the museum found itself in a financial crisis because it depended largely on state funding and replacing such major budget cuts would not be easy. The museum became aggressive in soliciting public support to close the budget gap and raised more than $160,000 with plans to host a black-tie gala fundraising event each of the next five years to diversity its financial support. The community was determined to save the ninety-eight-year-old museum. According to the museum director, "We're not going anywhere."[17]

In England, museums at the Museums Association Conference discussed how they dealt with major funding cuts and closures in a session entitled "Radical Future: Saving the Museum." The Birmingham Museums Trust discussed how that organization responded to a proposal by the Birmingham City Council to reduce the organization's budget by £850,000 in one year. In response, the Trust initiated and launched a campaign called the #SaveBhamMuseums campaign, designed to solicit funds from the general public and other stakeholders to provide financial support to diversify funding for the city's museums. The Trust decided to take a positive tone and convince the council that they "had the public's support and that is what the council needed to see." While the

Council did not agree to revoke the budget reduction, it did agree to spread the £850,000 reduction over two years instead of one, thus giving the museums time to raise additional funds and prepare for the ultimate funding reduction. In another presentation, the Ludlow Museum Resource Centre responded to a council decision to eliminate all museum staff and replace them with only one part-time employee. The museum began a "Friends" campaign to reverse the council's decision and solicit private funds to minimize the impact of the cuts. While the Museum generated additional funds to help support its continued operation, the council did not reverse its decision.[18]

Old Sturbridge Village (OSV) in Massachusetts found itself in serious financial trouble in the early 2000s. The Village experienced a major decline in attendance, reflecting the national trend among institutions of its type, from a high of 500,000 visitors in 1973 to about 265,000 in 2005. Since over 80 percent of its operating income was reliant on attendance-related sources, the loss of visitation dealt a devastating blow to Sturbridge's finances.[19] As a result, deficits increased; the endowment shrank; the operation of the Oliver Wright Tavern and Lodges ceased; the Education Center closed; costumed interpreters were replaced with signage; debt grew; wages were frozen; and many staff departed.[20]

The Village was on the brink of collapse when a new CEO was hired in 2007. Then came the financial collapse of 2008. The new leadership recognized that the culture at OSV had to change because "trustees always thought that admissions could cover expenses." The new CEO spent most of his first year developing a fundraising program.[21] Under disciplined leadership, OSV slowly bounced back, reversed downward attendance trends, and began an aggressive fundraising program.

One of the keys to OSV's success was diversifying revenue streams by emphasizing more engagement in fundraising by the board of trustees. The Village also broadened its appeal and focused on giving visitors memorable experiences.[22] In addition, the Village developed its own solar field, reopened the Education Center, and resumed ownership and operation of the Reeder Family Lodge and Oliver Wright Tavern. It also established Old Sturbridge Academy, a charter public school, and entered into a contractual agreement to manage the daily operations of the Coggeshall Farm Museum.

The prescription for financial success seems obvious from these examples: Develop a range of funding sources *before* a crisis sets in without over-reliance on too few sources that, if grossly reduced or eliminated, would result in the closure of the museum. It stands to reason that the more sources of funding an institution has, the less likely the loss of one source would have on financial stability, but diversification is not that simple.

The essence of revenue diversification is that it recognizes that relying on one primary revenue sources is a risky proposition, and finding and balancing several sources of income—contributed income, investment income and earned income—is preferable because together they provide a more stable cash flow; each will moderate any downturns or under-performance by the other. Diversification reduces exposure to risk and minimizes potential loss, especially when major sources are relatively evenly balanced. For example, the financial devastation caused by an overreliance on admissions at Old Sturbridge Village was mitigated when it rebalanced its funding portfolio by focusing more on contributions and fundraising and various entrepreneurial activities in addition to earned income. Thus OSV began to reduce—not eliminate—potential volatility and risk by allocating more time and resources to other income streams.

On the surface, this makes perfect sense, but in practice there are many considerations that inform whether diversification is the right move for individual museums, and how much and what kind of diversification is appropriate because each revenue source brings its own unique constraints of costs, time, and focus.

While it seems that diversifying revenue streams is always a good, sensible move, it requires careful thought and consideration. The first thing is to define why diversification matters to an organization. The answer differs from organization to organization. Does it mean asset growth, limiting market volatility, creating revenues for program growth, or supporting existing levels of ongoing operations? Does it mean expanding what an organization is already doing or entering into an en-tirely new line of business? And what does it mean with regard to alloca-tion of resources—is the museum willing to shift staff and money to de-velop new revenue streams and how will that impact available resources from existing revenue programs? Diversification needs to be approached cautiously.

In an article entitled "Is Diversification of Revenue Good for Nonprofit Health?" authors Mark Hager and Chia Ko Hung skillfully summarize from many studies the essential concerns of revenue diversification. They analyze both the upsides and downsides of diversification and distill the compelling arguments for and against.[23]

THE CASE FOR DIVERSIFICATION

The essential case for diversification is that it provides institutions with a degree of *flexibility*. This is what we usually think about when we think of diversification. Unfortunately, the future is not predictable, and many things happen that might jeopardize one major revenue stream. The authors suggest that there are two main types of uncertainty that affect an organization. The first is "environmental" or external change, which includes such things as major inclement weather conditions (e.g., a summer of rain is likely devastating for outdoor museums), dramatic downturns in the economy (people are less likely to attend fee-based museums if they are unemployed), civil unrest, or perhaps highway construction and detours that make it more difficult for visitors to access museums and their programs. The other uncertainty is more "personal" or inward change (in that it relates directly to specific organizations) when an institution's revenue stream might "just dry up." This is when funders reduce or eliminate their funding in favor of other priorities, grants are no longer forthcoming, or earned income initiatives are no longer productive at former levels.

Common sense tells us that if an institution relies on one major source—such as foundation funding—and for whatever reason that support is no longer forthcoming, an existential crisis ensues and may even be fatal for the continued operation of the museum. But if an institution relies on two or three major, unrelated sources—say, foundations and earned income—when one source dries up, it may not necessarily mean a death blow to the organization, although still serious. Diversification is, as the authors note, a "hedge against uncertainty."

An example of an institution that did not "hedge against uncertainty" was when the Big Idea Centre, dubbed the "Museum of Scottish Invention," opened in 2000 with the expectation that it could survive exclusively on earned income. As the museum sank further and further in debt as it relied largely on earned income, it was clear that this source alone could not support the Centre. It eventually closed in 2003.[24]

The second major reason for diversification is that it provides a level of *autonomy.* This means that an institution is not tied to one source of funding, which, in many cases, prescribes how money is spent and how an organization performs. Organizations, in essence, are doing what funders tell them to do with funding. But with unrestricted funds from such things as annual fund or earned income to supplement grant/foundation funding, institutions have more control over how they spend money, and there are fewer constraints. This provides more organizational freedom. Limited funding sources may keep an organization from properly representing how they fulfill their missions because of limitations or restrictions on how funds are used. Theoretically, organizations may find themselves in a position in which they apply for funding because they know a project is likely to be funded, rather than it being an institutional priority. In essence, the funders are calling the shots.

The last major reason in favor of diversification has to do with what the authors describe as *community embeddedness*. Community embeddedness is another term for social capital. Social capital is defined as "the value derived from positive connections between people."[25] Social capital is about perceptions that constituencies have of the museum and how they view its legitimacy—Hager and Hung suggest that social capital is "one part visibility, one part credibility, and one part networking."[26] It is also about the relationships that are developed and the reputation or standing the museum has earned. One of the ways a museum can earn social capital is through diversifying its sources of funding. For example, by initiating a broad-based capital campaign or even an annual fund program, museums expose themselves to potentially new audiences and supporters and thus increase their visibility and reputation. One can argue that limiting revenue streams not only limits revenue sources, but it also limits an institution's standing and importance in the community and thus its enduring value.

THE CASE AGAINST DIVERSIFICATION

Activities with the greatest potential returns are often the ones that carry the highest level of risk. U.S. Treasury Bonds, for example, earn relatively little income on an annual basis, but are safe investments. Investing in high-risk investments, on the other hand, while potentially quite lucrative, often carry the highest risk because they can be more speculative. They may produce big returns, but they may not. The key is balancing risk and reward. Anytime new revenue streams are pursued, they bring with them a certain amount of *risk and vulnerability*. A museum store may or may not be a good investment because there is considerable upfront investment (inventory, facility, staffing, and other operational costs) and the return is not guaranteed, or it may not show positive cash flow for years. Diversifying income requires that organizations look very carefully at the cost and benefits and determine the level of risk it wishes to carry or is capable of absorbing. Incurring too much risk may force the organization into a position in which it is far worse off than before it initiated the diversification program.

The authors also cite *Crowd-Out of Private Donations* as another potential downside of diversification. This means that a successful new revenue stream may be perceived as eliminating the need for personal donations. In other words, one revenue stream suffers because the new revenue stream is so successful. For example, if the museum opens a new café and store and an individual patronizes both, he may feel that he has adequately supported the museum and no longer needs to provide an annual fund gift. Crowd-out often happens with membership programs when individuals perceive the membership as their gift, and thus see no reason to give an annual fund gift—but the annual fund gift, in fact, is financially better for the museum because it does not have the overhead costs of servicing memberships. When blended together, one revenue source may influence the other, and must be looked at in terms of how they interact with the overall portfolio of revenue streams.

The last potential downside of revenue diversification is that it will likely bring *Increased Administrative Costs.* Getting into new lines of revenue-producing business brings both upfront and ongoing operational costs. Renting museums for private functions can produce significant income, but one must be mindful that such an enterprise may require increased staff to schedule and coordinate rentals, as well as incurring costs for software, maintenance, advertising, promotional costs, bookkeeping, security, and more. It is easy and understandable to be excited at the prospect of generating new sources of income, but as the saying goes, "it takes money to make money." It also takes additional degrees of operational complexity and stress as new programs are added to the operations of the museum. And when organizations are unable to properly support a new revenue initiative, it puts increased burdens on existing staff and budgets. As a result, it may dilute the quality and effectiveness of the overall revenue program. Sometimes the administrative costs are immediate, but the payoff may be longer term—such as the development of a museum retail sales operation that requires significant upfront costs. Realizing profit could potentially take several years. Can the organization afford to risk these resources? The trick, of course, is to maximize the revenue potential while minimizing the associated costs. The cost-benefit needs to be carefully analyzed.[27]

SUMMARY

Every organization has unique levels of risk tolerance, resources, expertise, and administrative capacity. They have their own comfort levels with existing revenue streams and unique requirements and needs for revenue mix. Everyone, however, tries to simultaneously blend the need for sustainable revenues with their mission imperatives to be accessible and serve the public. They try to minimize risk and maximize net revenues. Diversification may very well be a logical and productive effort, but some essential questions should be asked before moving forward.

Nonprofits compete for limited resources in an environment that is always changing. It makes sense not to rely too heavily on one major source of funding and instead spread the risk across several revenue streams. Yet there are decided downsides in diversification if these initiatives are not carefully considered. Thoughtful analysis and consideration are key, and there is no one solution for every organization.

ORGANIZATIONS THAT ENJOY SUCCESS:

Fully understand the reasons for diversification and know how success will be measured.

Analyze existing revenue streams, determine where there may be over-reliance, and decide how to reallocate resources to rebalance revenue streams.

Know when the time is right to diversify to ensure sufficient resources and focus.

Understand that diversification may shift existing resources of time, money, and focus from other revenue streams.

Know their level of risk tolerance and ability to absorb short-term expenditures to generate long-term gains.

Make efforts to maximize diversification with existing resources and limited funds to minimize risk.

Know their own "unfair advantages" and how to leverage them to diversify revenue streams.

Recognize the wisdom of proceeding carefully, starting small, and growing organically to minimize risk.

NOTES

1. Ford W. Bell, "How Are Museums Supported Financially in the U.S.?," Embassy of the United States of America (Washington, DC), https://static.america.gov/up loads/sites/8/2016/03/You-Asked-Series_How-Are-Museums-Supported-Finan cially-in-the-US_English_Lo-Res_508.pdf.
2. Mike Boehm, "MOCA faces serious financial problems," *Los Angeles Times*, November 19, 2008, https://www.latimes.com/entertainment/arts/la-et-moca19 -2008nov19-story.html.
3. Simon Thomsen, "A $250,000 anonymous donation has saved Victoria's Castlemaine Art Museum from closure," *Business Insider Australia*, August 3, 2017, https://www.businessinsider.com.au/a-250000-anonymous-donation-has-saved -victorias-castlemaine-art-museum-from-closure-2017-8.
4. Robin Pogrebin and Zachary Small, "Selling Art to Pay the Bills Divides the Nation's Museum Directors," *New York Times*, March 19, 2021, www.nytimes.com/2021/03/19 /arts/design/deaccession-museum-directors.html.
5. "Revised Collection Transfer Plan," Philadelphia History Museum at the Atwater Kent, November 13, 2019, http://www.philadelphiahistory.org/wp-content/up loads/2019/11/Collection-Transfer-Plan-2019.-11.-13.pdf.
6. Jacey Fortin, "The Philadelphia History Museum Is Closing Its Doors (Maybe for Good)," *New York Times*, June 30, 2018, https://www.nytimes.com/2018/06/30/us /philadelphia-history-museum-close.html.
7. "Revised Collection Transfer Plan," Philadelphia History Museum at the Atwater Kent.
8. Kelly Heyboer, "N.J. Museum of Agriculture to shut down due to state budget cuts," *NJ Advance Media*, March 31, 2019, https://www.nj.com/news/2011/02/new_jer sey_museum_of_agricultu.html.

9. "New Jersey Museum of Agriculture 2005 Convention," State of New Jersey Department of Agriculture, accessed May 9, 2021, https://www.nj.gov/agriculture /conventions/2005/agmuseumres.html.

10. "New Jersey Museum of Agriculture 2006 Convention," State of New Jersey Department of Agriculture, accessed May 9, 2021, https://www.nj.gov/agriculture /conventions/2006/agmuseumres.html.

11. "History," State Historical Society of North Dakota Foundation, accessed May 10, 2021, https://www.statehistoricalfoundation.org/history/.

12. Bernard Schoenburg, "Illinois State Museum closing would be devastating, advocate says," *State Journal-Register*, June 10, 2015, https://www.sj-r.com/article/20150610 /news/150619927.

13. Dave Alexander, "Johns Hopkins to Acquire Newseum Building in Washington, DC," *Johns Hopkins University HUB*, January 25, 2019, https://hub.jhu.edu/2019/01/25 /johns-hopkins-newseum-purchase-washington-dc/.

14. "Visit a Historic Working Mill," Hanford Mills Museum, accessed May 9, 2021, https://www.hanfordmills.org/visit-a-historic-workingmill/.

15. "Hanford Mills 2021–2023 Strategic Plan" (internal document, Hanford Mills Museum, 2020), 14–18.

16. Michael Hutchins, "Sherman Museum funding cut unless it finds additional sources," *Herald Democrat*, September 16, 2019, https://www.heralddemocrat.com /news/20190916/sherman-museum-funding-cut-unless-it-finds-additional-sources.

17. Aubrey McCall, "The Panhandle-Plains Historical Museum given a chance to prosper amid financial crisis," KFDA News, January 31, 2019, https://www.newschan nel10.com/2019/01/31/panhandle-plains-historical-museum-given-chance-pros per-amid-financial-crisis/.

18. Simon Stephens, "Saving the Museum," *Museums Association*, November 5, 2015, https:// www.museumsassociation.org/museums-journal/news/2015/11/05112015-fight ing-the-cuts/.

19. Astrid Wood, "Endangered Museums: The Viability of Living History Museums in the Modern Era" (PhD diss., Hampshire College, 2006).

20. James Connally (Old Sturbridge Village Coordinator of Interns and Fellows), interview by Brian Alexander, November 15, 2019.

21. James Donahue (Old Sturbridge Village President/ CEO), interview by Brian Alexander, November 15, 2019.

22. Ibid.

23. Mark Hager and ChiaKo Hung, "Is Diversification of Revenue Good for Nonprofit Financial Health?" *Nonprofit Quarterly*, October 1, 2020, https://nonprofitquarterly.org /is-diversification-of-revenue-good-for-nonprofit-financial-health/.

24. The Newsroom, "The Big Idea: Scotland's millennium project doomed to fail," *Scotsman*, August 9, 2016, https://www.scotsman.com/whats-on/arts-and-entertain ment/big-idea-scotlands-millennium-project-doomed-fail-1470279.

25. Rick L. Mask, "What Is Social Capital and Why Is It So Important?" Southern New Hampshire University, November 19, 2019, https://www.snhu.edu/about-us/news room/2019/11/what-is-social-capital.

26. Mark Hager and ChiaKo Hung, "Is Diversification of Revenue Good for Nonprofit Financial Health?"

27. Ibid.

5

Expanding When Ready

Growth and expansion are heady times for museums. Anticipation over the construction of a long-awaited new building or the addition of a much-needed exhibition wing creates unprecedented levels of pride and enthusiasm. Heightened levels of interest and excitement galvanize involvement from donors, members of the community, businesses, foundations, and the general public. Announcements of major gifts, participation by high-profile and wealthy donors, and promises of new and improved services all create palpable anticipation for a much-publicized grand opening and ribbon cutting.

The museum's profile is raised, and news outlets are filled with exciting stories describing expansion plans and progress. The museum is perceived as being "on the move"—growing its level of services, making spaces more accessible and attractive, allowing for more programming, expanding opportunities for increased exhibitions, and developing new means of generating revenue. It is an exhilarating time as the museum embraces the future.

EXPANSION ACTIVITY ABOUNDS

There is no shortage of expansion activity in the museum world, with major projects recently completed or planned by a wide range of organizations, such as the Museum of Modern Art; the Virginia Museum of Fine Arts; the Asheville Art Museum; the Connecticut Science Center; the National Postal Museum; the Metropolitan Museum of Art; the Westchester Children's Museum; the Anchorage Museum; the Colby College Art Museum; the National Railroad Museum; the Nelson-Atkins Museum of Art; the National Museum of the US Air Force; the American Museum of Natural History; the Holocaust Museum Houston; and the Motown Museum—and this is a short list. In Chicago alone, during the period 1994–2008, $869 million was spent on cultural institution building projects.[1]

During 2020, numerous major expansion projects were planned by museums throughout the world. The Munch Museum in Oslo moved from its original, much smaller facility to a new, thirteen-floor, 280,000-square-foot building that houses its collection of 1,150 Munch paintings and eighteen thousand prints at a cost of $293 million. The Philadelphia Museum of Art was nearing completion of the transformation of much of its original space and the addition of 90,000 square feet of new galleries and public spaces at a cost of $525 million. And the Crystal Bridges Museum of American Art converted a former cheese factory in Bentonville, Arkansas, into a new 62,000-square-foot contemporary art satellite facility called the Momentary.[2]

While most expansions in recent years trend mostly toward art museums, and are generally larger projects, they are not exclusively so. The American Museum of Natural History; the North Dakota Heritage Center; the Connecticut Science Center; the Motown Museum; the Holocaust Museum of Houston; and the Natural History Museum of Los Angeles are planning expansions. Even smaller organizations such as the National Corvette Museum; the St. Petersburg Museum of History; the Experience Children's Museum; and the Cody Firearms Museum are getting in on the act and feel the time is right to expand. There are so many expansions in recent years that it is nearly impossible to provide a complete list. New expansions are happening seemingly each day.

THE LURE OF EXPANSION

There is no one reason for expansion. Sometimes it is purely an expansion of existing operations to make the museum function more efficiently, accommodate growth, or perhaps respond to the need to attract new audiences or help sustain existing ones. In other cases, the need to stay relevant and keep pace with competitors drives expansion, especially as visitor expectations rise and technology changes the face of museum presentation. Expansion may also be driven by the need to generate new revenues and better position the museum for financial sustainability. Lastly, it is often an effort to modernize or even rebrand what seems like a tired, lifeless museum.

New construction, of course, quickly redefines an organization and gives it an improved, or even new, identity for itself and supports the economic development of existing and new locations. This was the case when the Guggenheim Museum expanded during the 1990s and created branches in such places as Las Vegas, Berlin, New York, and Bilbao, where the Guggenheim Bilbao opened in 1997.[3] The Guggenheim Bilbao was, according to author Paul Werner, "the visual centerpiece of a master plan for the economic redevelopment of the Basque Region."[4] Similar to this is the Strong National Museum of Play and the role it is playing in the redevelopment plan for downtown Rochester, New York. The museum is the driving force for the "Neighborhood of Play," a revitalization effort that includes many new attractions and gives both the city and the museum an expanded identity and significant economic impact.[5]

Expansion does not mean only physical expansion. It often means growth of operational capacity within the same facility footprint or an expansion of programming activities and other initiatives. These expansions are generally lower key and less dramatic and evolve over a period of time. Many times they are episodic, such as new programming or exhibitions, and are made possible by one-time funding with no appreciable long-term impact or commitment.

Regardless of the motivation or need, embarking on a major expansion must be carefully considered. The repercussions, especially the financial ones, are far-reaching. Dreams and aspirations must be carefully translated into reasonable, well-calculated planning. If not, the expansion impacts the museum in unexpected ways and creates the potential for an existential financial crisis. For example, one new museum in the South opened its new 43,000-square-foot facility in 1996. Once opened, it struggled with visitation and operating revenues, achieved only a fraction of its attendance projections, and by 2011 was forced to close permanently.[6] As Robin Pogrebin of the *New York Times* has written, "If it's hard to raise money for new buildings, it's even harder raising money to sustain them."[7]

When organizations believe that expansion may be a one-time opportunity, there is often an urge to overexpand and try to incorporate as many new features into the facility as possible. There are cost savings of scale, of course, and although each additional foot of expansion might be relatively less expensive to build, it creates increased financial commitment for ongoing operations for which the museum may not be ready. As a result, the museum expands well beyond its ability to fund both the expansion and subsequent operational costs.

Optimistic over expansion leaves little room for error or the unexpected. It can be difficult to slow, or even delay, expansion once the wheels are set into motion. It becomes seemingly impossible to turn back and equally difficult to move forward. Expectations are high, funds have been contributed, and work has commenced, but additional or unexpected costs stretch financial capacity to the breaking point. Perhaps the project was simply beyond institutional means in the first place or operational projections were too optimistic. Organizations soon find themselves in an untenable position. Expansion isn't something to take on without carefully understanding the pitfalls of attempting to grow too much, too soon.

THE NEED TO STAY RELEVANT

Staying relevant and responsive to an audience's changing needs is a full-time job. Losing relevance can happen virtually overnight, especially in a world in which there is constant technological change and increased levels of sophistication and expectations from museum audiences. It is essential to keep pace with these changes if a museum is to stay competitive. No matter how popular or profitable programs and services are, there is a life cycle to most programs or products, and if an institution does not anticipate and address these changes, it will find itself in trouble.[8]

Especially for relatively small institutions, expansion is a challenging notion. Limits to existing capacity keep them from adequately addressing growing visitor expectations, and scarce finances and relatively small fundraising constituencies make it difficult to think about growth that might attract new audiences and provide opportunities for revenue generation. These organizations operate so close to the financial edge that they cannot realistically think about the expense and risk of expansion when they are consumed by the everyday demands of just keeping the museum open. Thus, most small museums expand modestly, if at all. And since their financial capacity is so small, the very institutions that desperately need to expand and upgrade their services and facilities are not able to do so. They are not able to compete and find it impossible to attract audiences, and as a result, financial sustainability is in doubt and, in some instances, they are forced to close. One museum in Tennessee closed temporarily in 2018 after thirty-six years because of its "old-school type" exhibitions and its inability to provide adequate funding to expand and improve its exhibitions. "They just haven't spent any money on that museum," said the president of the museum friends group.[9]

Spencer Johnson put it succinctly in his classic *Who Moved My Cheese?* when discussing the necessity of change for survival: "If you do not change, you can become extinct."[10] Yet, even if a museum is aware of the need for change, it may not be able to make the changes necessary to achieve viability. One battlefield museum closed and its contents were sold at auction in 2014 after over fifty years of operation because the museum was not able to "keep making changes and look at different ways of doing things," according to its director.[11]

ACCEPTABLE RISK AND "ONE TOE" EXPANSION

Growth is essential if museums are to retain a competitive edge and stay relevant in the marketplace, but in a field in which financial resources are often scarce, it takes courage to assume significant levels of risk. Expansion must done in a careful, regulated fashion, but even then there are no guarantees for success. It is important not to be swayed by plans that are too grand and projections of financial success that are too aggressive.

Museums must recognize that quick, dramatic changes are sometimes financially disastrous and programmatically impossible. Giant leaps of expansion are potentially dangerous to organizational stability and may well jeopardize an institution's financial future. The question is, how much risk is an institution willing to incur and what happens if projections for funding are not realized?

It is tempting to pursue major expansion because of the fear of being left behind, but sometimes risks are just too aggressive. Instead, it is advisable to proceed in a cautious, organic fashion—always adapting, changing, improving, and testing with the big-picture implications in mind. Apple constantly changed its products as technology changed and grew accordingly; it did not jump from the Macintosh computer to the Apple Watch overnight. There were plenty of developments in between that paved the way and informed successful, organic growth.[12]

Like Apple, museums are well advised to be in a constant state of change and responsiveness to their customers, but it is more prudent to make a midstream course correction and learn from small mistakes than to proceed directly to a grand plan that, if unsuccessful, will have disastrous consequences financially and programmatically. The trick is to be realistic and know the limits of the museum's ability to expand and grow. There may be pressures or dreams that are simply unrealistic. The museum may end up in a place far worse than before expansion.

Capital expansion in particular creates a major operational commitment. It means new, ongoing funding for programming, operations, exhibitions, maintenance, and other expenses to which the institution has committed itself for the long term. Committing to an institutional physical expansion is one of the most significant and far-reaching decisions a museum makes and must be done with extreme care and thoughtful planning. The potential for disaster is high, and the stakes are considerable. Successful expansion usually happens only if it is done in a careful, regulated fashion.[13]

The Shedd Aquarium in Chicago created a separate endowment, *in advance*, to support operating costs for future expansion activities. The Aquarium prepared itself to support the future without an overreliance on optimistic revenue projections. According to the executive vice president at the time, "I definitely would not say that any one of us rests on the laurels of 'We have one of the best collections in the world; if you build it they will come.' No," he notes, "they won't."[14]

It is a natural instinct to want to grow, improve, and get bigger and better. But it isn't necessarily the most prudent course of action. Bigger doesn't always mean better; sometimes it makes matters worse because operations and programs are diluted by the expansion. At the same time, if done wisely in an incremental way, it provides the means to grow audiences and revenues and achieve other institutional goals. Expanding programs, services, and facilities carries inherent risks, but so does allowing an organization to remain stagnant when it needs to retain a competitive edge and continue to attract visitors. "There is obviously great enthusiasm for making (cultural institutions) bigger and better. It's well-intended, to improve the institution," according to museum consultant Barry Lord of Toronto—but boards sometimes forget to ask: "Is the market showing that much demand?"[15]

Tom Peters addresses the issue of growth and expansion in his classic study of business excellence, *In Search of Excellence*, in which he notes that the excellent companies expand "in manageable steps . . . and clearly contain the risks. And are willing to get out if it doesn't work."[16] According to Peters, "The excellent companies don't test new waters with both feet. Better yet, when they stuck a toe in new waters and failed, they terminated the experiment quickly."[17]

It is difficult to extract an organization from expansion if it jumps in with both feet; it is safer and more prudent to do it one toe at a time. When an organization has relatively little margin for error, as is the case with most nonprofit museums, the "one toe" approach is sensible because the nature of such a measured approach is not irreversible or life-threatening to the institution. Naturally, the lucky museum that has most of its funding in place may take on a more aggressive expansion at one time.

An example of "one toe" expansion is the Strong National Museum of Play in Rochester, New York. The museum was established in 1971 as the Margaret Woodbury Strong Museum and originally presented itself largely as a decorative arts and toy museum. Throughout its history, it underwent almost-continuous strategic planning, careful market research, a commitment to change with shifting audience needs and interests, and a laser focus on exploiting its strengths. This thoughtful and ongoing planning allowed the museum to expand both physically and programmatically in a careful, responsible fashion. In addition to revising its mission with more focus on the concept of play and directing its effort more toward family groups and interactive programs, the museum expanded its footprint to 282,000 square feet with a $37 million expansion in 2004–2006, changed its name and branding, and now averages 550,000 visitors per year with over sixteen thousand member-households.[18]

In recent years, the Strong continues to grow; it now includes the National Toy Hall of Fame and the International Center for the History of Electronic Games, it publishes the *American Journal of Play*. The museum is currently engaged in an expansion project that provides the museum with an additional 90,000 square feet in new interactive exhibits and houses the Strong's World Video Game Hall of Fame. This expansion is the driving force for the "Neighborhood of Play," a revitalization effort in the downtown area surrounding the museum. Expected to attract an additional 400,000 guests, the neighborhood will include a mix of retail properties, a "playfully themed" 1,000-car parking garage, and a family-friendly hotel. It is expected to create an economic impact of $130 million per year in downtown Rochester.[19]

TYPES OF EXPANSION

There are different types of growth and expansion, and it is important to understand the type of growth most appropriate for a museum in its institutional life cycle. Shooting for the fences too early may not be appropriate because the institution may not be ready for a major physical expansion; instead, it may just wish to expand and improve program offerings and maximize use of existing facilities. Expansion is not a one-size-fits-all proposition, and it is not always about new brick-and-mortar construction.

In his article "Four Dimensions of Nonprofit Growth," Mark Fulopon outlines four distinct categories of institutional growth for nonprofits:[20]

OPERATIONAL GROWTH

This phase of growth addresses the need for an organization to continue its current level of work, but to do so in ways that are more effective and efficient. The idea is to provide services at a higher level of quality. This begins with an assessment of true operational needs and costs that allow the museum to function at a higher level. This may mean such things as improving salaries to attract and retain employees, offering professional training opportunities for staff, developing new revenue streams, improving existing infrastructure, or upgrading technology to enhance operational efficiencies. It simply means upgrading the quality and efficiencies of operational activities and determining ways in which work can be done better.

An excellent example of operational growth is that undertaken by the Cape Ann Museum in Gloucester, Massachusetts. Numerous initiatives identified in its Strategic Plan 2010–2016 became the centerpiece of a $5 million capital campaign. The key components of its growth were not building expansion or new construction. Instead, the museum focused on making better and more efficient use of its existing resources. The project included upgrading security and HVAC systems; adding curatorial and other essential personnel; improving the care of collections; realigning and reinterpreting its central gallery; installing new lighting and flooring in galleries; installing new signage; and further growing the acquisitions fund and operating endowment. Although perhaps not as glamorous or attention-grabbing as a major physical expansion, the project represents solid, responsible initiatives to maximize resources and position the museum for its next stage of growth.

By pursuing projects such as these, museums may differentiate themselves from their competitors by focusing on the high quality of their presentations. In the case of the Cape Ann Museum, it is positioning itself for the future without mortgaging away that very future. And when existing customers know the museum is working to continually improve itself and its programs, they are likely to remain loyal and increasingly prideful of the institution. The museum will likely attract new customers as well.[21]

PROGRAM GROWTH

Once the fully funded operation is in place, the museum begins to think about the *growth* of existing programs and services. Again, determining the true cost of existing services is an essential part of thinking about program growth. Examples of program growth include such things as expanding public hours, making programs more available to audiences, hiring new staff to administer increased workloads, serving more visitors, and generally expanding the reach and impact of the museum's programs and services. Fulopon argues that the key "drivers" of program growth are plans that respond to a compelling need for the growth and evidence that programs and services are effectively meeting those needs. In other words, there must be a solid reason for the program growth. In this type of expansion, an organization is usually at the point where it has done as much as possible with its existing resources and must expand programmatically if it is to continue to be successful. It does not mean major physical expansion. Undertaking this type of growth generally carries less inherent risk and complexity and typically is more predictable. For example, expanding the accessibility of existing programs to new audiences will not create an existential crisis if it does not work.

The Museum of Science in Boston blended several stages of Fulopon's model into one major $284-million project. The goal of the project was for the museum "to become the leading science center worldwide in expanding the public's access to, understanding of, and critical thinking around engineering technology, and the sciences," according to the museum's president. The museum initiated operational growth by transforming the lobby, box office, concourse, and entrance, as well as making enhancements to the facility by adding solar panels. It also transformed nearly half of its 130,000 square feet of galleries, as well as the Charles Hayden

Planetarium, making it New England's most technologically advanced digital theater. It grew its programs by establishing the National Center for Technological Literacy, the Gordon Science and Technology Center, and the nation's first rooftop wind-turbine lab. It also unveiled the new major exhibitions, *The Hall of Human Life* and *The Science Behind Pixar*.[22]

PROGRAM EXPANSION

This phase is about expanding programs and services into new areas and usually requires significant financial resources, new competencies, and additional infrastructure. This includes additional startup costs, as well as ongoing operating costs. It must determine if the development of new infrastructure justifies the initial construction costs as well as the long-term operating costs. This level is like creating a completely new business with new customers and revenue bases. Because of significant new operating costs, it cannot reasonably be assimilated into the ongoing budget or current levels of operation. The trick in doing this is not to add new programs, services, and facilities before careful consideration of the attendant costs of sustaining these new activities. Otherwise, existing revenue streams are "cannibalized" in the service of the new program expansion and dilute revenues to the point that expansion costs hurt the effectiveness of *all* the museum's programs and services.

An example of program expansion is the Museum of Modern Art in New York (MOMA), which completed a new 47,000-square-foot addition on the former site of the American Folk Art Museum. At a cost of $450 million, the expansion was designed to relieve pressure on growing MOMA crowds, expand exhibitions, and increase annual attendance by one-half million people. With the addition of many new galleries and a restaurant, the philosophy of the expansion was that adding space would attract many more people—that which transportation experts refer to as "induced demand." Certainly, an expansion of $450 million brings with it considerable risk, but given MOMA's history of organic growth over the years, as well as its consistently growing attendance, location, and reputation, the success of the expansion is probably a good bet.[23]

Another example of a major program and facility expansion is the Peabody Essex Museum in Salem, Massachusetts. The Peabody Museum and Essex Institute merged in 1992, and its recent 40,000-square-foot expansion is believed to make it the ninth-largest art museum in North America.[24] The expansion includes a 5,000-square-foot garden and another $16 million in planned exhibition installations. These initiatives are all designed to make the Peabody Essex "an art museum experience unlike that found anywhere else." The 2019 expansion was on the heels of a new 120,000-square-foot Collection Center, which opened in 2018 and houses a library, conservation lab, photo studio, digitization studio, collections storage, and offices. By any standard, the Peabody Essex expansion activities are aggressive, but they are doing it with careful consideration of funding sustainability. Concurrent with the expansion, the museum is working to provide a "new financial model" for American art museums that provides for twice the average endowment support for museum operations. The goal is to build an endowment that is capable of funding 60 percent of its operations as opposed to the average 30 percent endowment support of art museums.[25]

Often institutions find themselves in a difficult place when they pursue major expansions before they are ready, or when the expansion grows beyond the institution's ability to complete it. They find themselves in financial trouble (mostly with building expansion projects) because they jumped into the initiative before they were adequately positioned to do so and were forced to postpone the project or abandon it entirely until a solution presented itself. Those organizations that focus on slower, more organic growth tend to have a higher rate of success.

This was the case with the Metropolitan Museum of Art in New York, which found itself struggling with operating deficits of nearly $40 million and the postponement of a $600-million wing in large part because of an aggressive expansion program that included overspending on the new MET Breuer building, borrowing heavily from the endowment, and pursuing a new wing before a solid financial plan and funding were in place. There was concern that the MET was too heavily focused on expansion and not enough on emphasizing the core programs that had made the museum great in the first place. It was simply a question of doing too much, too soon.[26]

PROGRAM REPLICATION

This level of growth happens when an organization decides that because it has been so successful in its current location, it is in its interests to expand its operation to another location outside its immediate geographic area. The important considerations of program replication, according to Fulopon, are for institutions to have a solid base and history of having a major impact in its geographical area, a strong history of success, and the knowledge that it can be replicated in another area with similar outcomes. It is also important to understand that there is the possibility of losing the "critical characteristics" of the replication if operations and funding become too diluted. There must be confidence that an organization can produce a similar impact or successful outcome (financially and programmatically) in another location. According to Fulopon, it is key for an organization to clearly understand the process of replication of its operation, to know in detail the cost of replicating it, and to determine how ongoing quality at the new location will be assured. There must be clear understanding of initial capital requirements as well as long-term operational funding.

The Guggenheim Museum in New York is an example of program replication when it determined to "pursue cultural dialogue and exchange around the world"[27] although it met with varying degrees of success. In 1997, it expanded internationally with the opening of the Guggenhem Museum Bilbao in Spain.[28] Considered to be an architectural masterpiece, the museum has been described as "seamlessly integrated into the urban context." The 350,000-square-foot site includes nineteen galleries for the exhibition of American and European painting and sculpture and has become an important part of the urban redevelopment efforts in the region. Partly subsidized by the Basque government, it is now one of the largest museums in Spain.

The Guggenheim also expanded into other areas of New York with the opening of the Guggenheim SoHo (1992–2001)[29] followed by an expansion into Germany with the opening of the Deutsche Guggenheim (1997–2013) funded by Deutsche Bank.[30] The Guggenheim also formed an alliance with the State Hermitage Museum of St. Petersburg, Russia, and opened the Guggenheim Hermitage in Las Vegas in October 2001 (closed 2008), and in the same year, it opened the 63,700-square-foot Guggenheim Las Vegas, but it closed after just over a year because of low attendance.[31]

The Guggenheim further pursued replication with the Guggenheim Rio, which was planned but never developed,[32] as was the Guggenheim Guadalahara.[33] The museum also made an unsuccessful attempt to develop the Guggenheim Helsinki in 2016. Many of these projects were stopped or abandoned because of high development costs and unsustainable operating projections.[34] The Guggenheim has also been at work on the 450,000-square-foot Guggenheim Abu Dhabi in the United Arab Emirates since 2006.[35]

Despite these setbacks, the Guggenheim still lists four museums on its website as a result of program replication: the Solomon R. Guggenheim Museum in New York; the Peggy Guggenheim Collection in Venice, Italy; the Guggenheim Bilbao in Bilbao, Spain; and the Guggenheim Abu Dhabi in the United Arab Emirates.[36]

BIG PLANS AND BIG PROJECTIONS

Every expansion project must have credible feasibility and business plans to carefully project capital expansion and operational costs as well as well-considered revenue projections. Those institutions that "borrowed conservatively, raised money ahead of times and projected realistic revenues" tend to be most successful.[37]

Many expansion projects such as those at the Asian Art Museum and the New Museum plan for increased operational costs and additional revenues (including endowment) as part of the overall expansion plan. This is because endowment fundraising by itself is typically difficult.[38]

Sometimes museums are deluded by their optimism for a project, rely too much on questionable revenue projections, and get ahead of themselves with their expansive plans. According to Michael Kimmelman, art and architecture critic of the *New York Times*, expansion is a reflection of a trend in art museums, who "now believe they need to go big or go home, vying for our divided attention."[39]

An example of this is when one major Midwest museum broke ground on a new wing in 2005 and apparently did not have a complete understanding of how much the project would ultimately cost. In the end it cost about $380 million, but the $162 million pledged when the project began was only about 43 percent of the total, well below the norm of 50 to 70 percent for such projects. As a consequence, the museum's total liabilities reached their highest level ever at $452 million. Then, when the wing opened, the economic downturn of 2008 hit, and the endowment lost a quarter ($224 million) of its value—which negatively affected its ability to fund the operations of the new wing. Although attendance projections grew significantly following construction of the wing, it soon reverted back to historical levels.[40]

In Philadelphia a growing museum decided to go big when it moved from a small space to a much larger building. The museum borrowed heavily to fund its expansion, and in 2015 it found itself $60 million in debt. The museum was well-attended and surpassed many of its visitation projections, but it did not achieve its operating revenue goals or fundraising projections, falling well below estimates. And when it sold the property on which it was originally located, the 2008 recession forced a sale well under half of the $8.5-million asking price. Between construction debts, failure of projected admissions, fundraising performance, and the cost of operating the expanded new facility, the museum found itself unable to pay its debt payments. In 2015, it filed for Chapter 11 bankruptcy, and bond holders received only a portion of the amount owed to settle the debt.[41] Since then it has been tightening its financial belt, reducing staff, increasing efficiencies, and "reinvigorating philanthropic outreach."[42]

Another museum announced it would delay for as much as seven years the expansion of a $600-million exhibition wing in favor of the need to first get its financial house in order. The museum's director noted the wisdom of first pursuing urgent maintenance projects (such as replacing a roofing system) and *then* formulating longer-term expansion projects "into a responsible master plan that matches our capacity with our ambition."[43]

A science and technology museum in Utah struggled when it opened in 2011 because its startup costs were more than planned. As a result, the museum found itself in significant debt, even after creditors forgave 20 percent of the debt and renegotiated the rest. The museum even took $600,000 in loans from employees and board members to fund operating expenses. In 2018 the museum had liabilities that exceeded assets by nearly $2 million, and the city in which it was located was forced to send the museum a formal letter of default for loan and utility bills owed the city.[44]

Optimistic financial projections fuel confidence during the period of actual expansion, but they can also create artificial hope for sustainability if the financial plan is unrealistically aggressive. When the excitement of the new project begins to fade and the operational realities begin to appear, serious problems reveal themselves. The early confidence of operational sustainability reveals itself as a much bigger challenge than originally imagined, takes longer than originally planned, or in some cases does not happen at all. Making matters worse are capital expansion cost over-runs. Then the museum finds itself in a difficult situation in which it has spent more than planned but revenues are less than anticipated. Soon the museum is saddled with unanticipated debt or is forced to make withdrawals from endowments, further eroding its revenue-producing capacity.

Many involved in major expansions or new construction often "lowball" projected operating expenses during a project's early phases, according to Adrian Ellis, director of AEA Consulting in New York. Ellis describes the fate of a now-defunct museum in Sheffield, England. After construction, mostly funded by Britain's lottery, the museum attracted only about a quarter of the visitation it projected and closed down in just over one year.[45] The same expansion that created an initial sense of institutional renewal and revitalization soon brought increased financial obligations less glamorous than capital expansion but necessary for day-to-day operation. Utilities must be paid, and buildings must be maintained, programmed, and secured. Loans also must be repaid. Expectations of constituencies become higher than ever, but finances are stretched to unprecedented levels. Ellis notes that the lack of proper planning for operations results in "living-dead institutions, zombies whose preoccupation is daily survival."[46]

THE IMPORTANCE OF CAREFUL PROJECTIONS

The decision to expand must be the result of careful planning and research. It is essential to thoroughly evaluate a wide range of factors, including projected capital and operating costs, likely return on investment, the logistics of expansion (how it will affect ongoing operations during expansion), funder readiness, consumer demand, and many other considerations. In general, a simple rule of thumb is that an institution should expand only if doing so will provide untapped opportunities and if the costs of doing so will not outweigh the advantages that are created.

The Newseum, which originally opened in 1997 in Rosslyn, Virginia, was so successful that the Freedom Forum, its principal funder, paid $100 million for a parcel of land in Washington, DC, and then took out $350 million in construction loans to develop a much-larger museum facility. When it did not realize revenue projections, the museum reduced expenses, made five rounds of staff cuts over ten years, and ran significant deficits. In 2015, the museum found itself caving under its financial burdens. In addition to funding its $61-million budget, it still owed over $300 million for the development and construction of the new nine-floor facility. There was real concern that the museum was not sustainable, and it was sold in 2018 to Johns Hopkins University for $372.5 million.[47]

On Long Island in New York, a new museum opened in 2002 and got off to a rocky start when it lagged behind expectations of both attendance and revenue. It was forced to scale back original attendance projections from 300,000 to 260,000 and then to 180,000. In its first year, it ran a $400,000 deficit, and the following year a deficit of $ 1.1 million was anticipated. Then, after only two years of operation, the museum asked Nassau County that its loan payment of $250,000 to cover operating expenses be deferred.[48]

SUCCESSFUL EXPANSION

There are many examples of expansion initiatives that have successfully grown the cultural imprint and reach of museums. The New Museum of New York recently announced that it had raised $79 million of a $89 million project. It wisely accounted for increased operational costs by allocating $63 million for construction and $26 million for operating endowment and cash reserves.[49] The Asian Art Museum in San Francisco announced in 2017 that it had raised $60 million of a $90-million goal, which included $38 million for new public spaces, $27 million for program and exhibition development, and $25 million for operating endowment.[50]

The Norton Museum of Art in West Palm Beach, Florida, recently completed a $100-million expansion with 50,000 new square feet of new exhibition space, classrooms, dining, gardens, and an auditorium, among other amenities.[51] The project exceeded its $100-million fund-raising goal by $10 million, anticipated increased operational costs, and even allowed for a $4-million endowment for the director's position.[52]

The Philadelphia Museum of Art's massive $525-million capital campaign, the largest capital expansion in its history, allocated about $233 million for actual capital improvements, but it supplemented that with $142 million in educational and technological initiatives, and most importantly, it designated $150 million for the museum's operating endowment—which, by standard calculations, would provide an additional $7.5 million or so in operating income each year, funds that presumably support the additional costs of the new programs and expansion.[53]

UNEXPECTED THINGS HAPPEN

Timing is everything in making the decision to expand. Changes in the economy, a domestic or international crisis, donor readiness, other capital projects underway or recently completed in the museum's geographical area, changing consumer tastes, and unexpected circumstances all have a direct impact on expansion. Unless an institution has unlimited funds, it must think strategically about when to expand. Even then, there is no guarantee of success because many things are simply beyond its control, regardless of how well it plans.

Sometimes unanticipated capital expenditures must be made when initial construction estimates are insufficient and plans for operational funding are "devoured by direct building costs," according to one museum official in Virginia. This museum saw original construction costs soar from $46 million to $66 million and was forced to terminate many of its staff members shortly after opening in 2008.[54]

One venerable museum in New England found itself in serious financial trouble in large part due to an expansion initiative in 2003, when it opened its new multipurpose visitor center. Designed to provide a more extensive and meaningful experience for visitors, the new center was completed at a cost of $19 million, nearly double the original cost projections.[55] The expansion included a large auditorium, a gift shop, a theater, classrooms, a café, and other visitor amenities. Despite increased costs of expansion, the museum continued the project, hoping that the expansion would eventually be a success and pay for itself.[56]

The museum soon found itself in financial distress because the project was heavily mortgaged; attendance projections did not materialize; energy costs were far more than anticipated; and it was later learned that a long-time employee had embezzled significant funds.[57] Then came the economic crisis of 2008. Even with banks forgiving millions in loans and the museum receiving additional assistance from the state government, it nearly closed in 2008. It was left with $5 million in debt, a significantly reduced staff, and limited means to fund payroll and other obligations. The museum came within three to four weeks of closing its doors.[58] In recent years, however, the museum has made impressive progress in turning around its financial challenges, and it has put itself back on a more solid financial foundation.[59]

PUBLIC EXPECTATIONS

Public expectations are high during expansion, and those who contributed to the program want to see demonstrable results from their investment. Disappointing the public and donors can have serious implications for ongoing relationships and future support. Commitments must be kept because they are part of the contract made between the museum and its public.

An art museum in California suspended a plan for a new $12-million building when its capital campaign did not generate anticipated funding and was unable to match a gift from a charitable trust. The new building was two decades into its planning but was forced to go "back to the drawing board" and focus first on growing membership and donors, encouraging community engagement, and maintaining its existing facility rather than expansion. As a result of the planned expansion and related costs, the museum's overall finances suffered, and it soon found itself in a precarious financial position at a time when expectations for new and exciting programs and services were high. The city intervened because it "had an expectation that there would be a new building," and it wanted the museum to succeed.[60]

In 2016 a science museum in Florida ran out of money before construction was complete on its major expansion project. It was unable to secure bank loans and make a $5 million payment for construction costs. The board of trustees was unable to get donors to honor existing pledges and generate new fundraising to complete the project. As a result, the lead donors of the project agreed to bail out the museum to complete the project, but only if the entire forty-one-member board of trustees resigned, which it did. Taxpayers had already contributed $160 million to the state-of-the-art project during its construction phase, and county officials reacted with "shock and horror" at the unexpected news of the project's financial crisis.[61]

SUMMARY

Many expansion efforts are successful and achieve their dreams, but others struggle to find their financial footing as they face major institutional crises caused by expansion. Capital expansion is often far more expensive than anticipated, and projections for attendance and revenues are often far less than originally projected.

Many museums have pursued expansion activities in recent years. Like businesses in the for-profit world, museums must constantly evolve to stay relevant and competitive in the marketplace. It is critical to proceed carefully, and thoughtfully consider the short- and long-term financial implications and not bet the very survival of the organization on anything less.

ORGANIZATIONS THAT ENJOY SUCCESS:

Look first at maximizing existing facilities before initiating major new expansion.

Grow organically, learn from small mistakes, and avoid excessive risk-taking.

Carefully consider both expansion and operating costs, often creating endowments as part of the capital expansion.

Don't get caught in overexpansion mode by trying to do too much, too soon.

Carefully evaluate the risks they are willing and able to take.

Know that there will be unexpected issues and costs and plan for them.

Make decisions in a calculated, businesslike fashion, not with emotions.

Manage constituent relations (donors, public, government etc.) and deliver what they promise.

NOTES

1. Heather Gillers and Jason Grotto, "Chicago museums reeling after spending sprees," *Chicago Tribune*, March 3, 2013, https://www.chicagotribune.com/news /ct-xpm-2013-03-13-ct-met-museum-finance-20130313-story.html.
2. Gareth Harris, "New Museums and Major Expansions Opening in 2020," *Art Newspaper*, January 1, 2020, https://www.theartnewspaper.com/preview/museums -popping-up-around-the-world.
3. Paul Werner, *Museum, Inc: Inside the Global Art World* (Prickly Paradigm Press, 2005), 1.
4. Werner, *Museum, Inc: Inside the Global Art World*, 51.
5. "Expansion Project," The Strong National Museum of Play, accessed February 15, 2020, https://www.museumofplay.org/expansion-campaign/expansion-project.
6. "Georgia Music Hall of Fame Museum and Education," Georgia Music Hall and Education Resources, accessed February 15, 2020, www.gamusichall.com/.
7. Mike Scutari, "Almost There: Key takeaways from a museum's successful capital campaign," *Inside Philanthropy*, August 6, 2019, https://www.insidephilanthropy.com /home/2019/8/3/the-new-museum-in-new-york-has-announced-details-of-its -63-million-expansion.
8. Robert Cordray, "10 Valid Reasons Why Businesses Should Always Be Expanding Their Product Portfolio," *Business 2 Community*, January 16, 2015, https://www .business2community.com/business-innovation/10-valid-reasons-businesses-al ways-expanding-product-portfolio-01126471.
9. Tom Charlier, "Mud Island's Mississippi River Museum Closes for Review," *Memphis Commercial Appeal*, July 5, 2018, https://www.commercialappeal.com/story /news/2018/07/05/mississippi-river-museum-closes/760691002/.
10. Spencer Johnson, *Who Moved My Cheese?* (G.P. Putnam's Sons, 1998), 46.
11. Chris Kaltenbach, "After 50-plus years, Gettysburg's Soldier's National Museum is a goner," *Baltimore Sun*, November 1, 2014, https://www.baltimoresun.com/travel/bs-ae -museum-20141101-story.html.

12. Robert Cordray, "10 Valid Reasons Why Businesses Should Always Be Expanding Their Product Portfolio," *Business 2 Community*, January 16, 2015, https://www.business2community.com/business-innovation/10-valid-reasons-businesses-always-expanding-product-portfolio-01126471.

13. "Capital Campaigns: Understanding the Basics," *DonorSearch*, accessed February 16, 2020, https://www.donorsearch.net/capital-campaigns-guide/.

14. Heather Gillers and Jason Grotto, "Chicago museums reeling after spending sprees," *Chicago Tribune*, March 3, 2013, https://www.chicagotribune.com/news/ct-xpm-2013-03-13-ct-met-museum-finance-20130313-story.html.

15. Gillers and Grotto, "Chicago museums reeling after spending sprees."

16. Thomas J. Peters and Robert H. Waterman, *In Search of Excellence* (Harper and Row Publishers, 1982), 301.

17. Thomas J. Peters and Robert H. Waterman, *In Search of Excellence* (Harper and Row Publishers, 1982), 299.

18. Amy Hollister Zarlengo, Gretchen Sullivan Sorin, and Lynne A. Sessions, "The Great Transformation at the Strong," *Case Studies in Cultural Entrepreneurship*, ed. AASLH, (Rowman & Littlefield, 2015).

19. "Expansion Project," The Strong National Museum of Play, accessed February 15, 2020, https://www.museumofplay.org/expansion-campaign/expansion-project.

20. Mark P. Fulop, "Four Dimensions of Nonprofit Growth," Facilitation and Process, accessed February 15, 2020, http://facilitationprocess.com/four-dimensions-of-nonprofit-growth/.

21. "Reaching Out, Strengthening Within," Cape Ann Museum Capital Campaign, Cape Ann Museum, accessed February 16, 2020, http://www.capeannmuseum.org/media/uploads/casestatement-web-pdf-rev-oct2013.pdf.

22. "Museum of Science, Boston closes $250 million Campaign, Topping Goal by $34 million," Museum of Science, June 19, 2015, https://www.mos.org/node/15735846.

23. Michael Kimmelman, "With a $450 Million Expansion, MoMA Is Bigger. Is That Better?" *New York Times*, October 9, 2019, https://www.nytimes.com/2019/10/09/arts/design/with-a-450-million-expansion-moma-is-bigger-is-that-better.html.

24. Jenn Stanley, "With Expansion, Peabody Essex Explores Complicated History of Museums," *ARTery*, September 24, 2019, https://www.wbur.org/artery/2019/09/24/peabody-essex-museum-expansion.

25. "PEM's Expansion Project," About PEM//Expansion, Peabody Essex Museum, accessed February 16, 2020, https://www.pem.org/about-pem/expansion.

26. Robin Pogrebin, "Is the Met Museum 'a Great Institution in Decline'?" *New York Times*, February 4, 2017, https://www.nytimes.com/2017/02/04/arts/design/met-museum-financial-troubles.html.

27. "Guggenheim Helsinki," Guggenheim, accessed February 16, 2020, https://www.guggenheim.org/guggenheim-helsinki.

28. "A Structure of Titanium, Glass and Limestone," The Building, Guggenheim Bilbao, accessed February 16, 2020, https://www.guggenheim-bilbao.eus/en/the-building/the-construction.

29. Carol Vogel, "Inside Art; Guggenheim Shrinks in SoHo," *New York Times*, February 5, 1999, https://www.nytimes.com/1999/02/05/arts/inside-art-guggenheim-shrinks-in-soho.html.

30. Alan Cowell, "New U.S. Sector in Berlin: Little Guggenheim Branch," *New York Times*, November 7, 1997, https://www.nytimes.com/1997/11/07/arts/new-u-s-sector-in-berlin-little-guggenheim-branch.html?pagewanted=2&src=pm.

31. Kristen Peterson, "Vegas, say goodbye to Guggenheim," *Las Vegas Sun,* April 10, 2008, https://lasvegassun.com/news/2008/apr/10/vegas-say-goodbye-guggenheim/.

32. Lee Rosenbaum, "More on Tom Krens from James Russell (and me)," CultureGrrl, *Arts Journal*, February 29, 2008, http://www.artsjournal.com/culturegrrl/2008/02/more_on_tom_krens_from_james_r.html.

33. Jason Edward Kaufman, "Why the Guggenheim Won't Open a Branch in Guadalajara," *Banderas News*, June 2008, http://www.banderasnews.com/0806/art-guggenheim.htm.

34. Lee Rosenbaum, "More on Tom Krens from James Russell (and me)," CultureGrrl, *Arts Journal*, February 29, 2008, http://www.artsjournal.com/culturegrrl/2008/02/more_on_tom_krens_from_james_r.html.

35. "Soloman R. Guggenheim Foundation Timeline," History, Guggenheim, accessed February 16, 2020, https://www.guggenheim.org/history/foundation.

36. The Guggenheim Museum, accessed February 16, 2020, https://www.guggenheim.org/.

37. Heather Gillers and Jason Grotto, "Chicago museums reeling after spending sprees," *Chicago Tribune*, March 3, 2013, https://www.chicagotribune.com/news/ct-xpm-2013-03-13-ct-met-museum-finance-20130313-story.html.

38. Gillers and Grotto, "Chicago museums reeling after spending sprees."

39. Michael Kimmelman, "With a $450 Million Expansion, MoMA Is Bigger. Is That Better?" *New York Times*, October 9, 2019, https://www.nytimes.com/2019/10/09/arts/design/with-a-450-million-expansion-moma-is-bigger-is-that-better.html.

40. Heather Gillers and Jason Grotto, "Chicago museums reeling after spending sprees," *Chicago Tribune*, March 3, 2013, https://www.chicagotribune.com/news/ct-xpm-2013-03-13-ct-met-museum-finance-20130313-story.html.

41. Jared Shelly, "Please Touch Museum Files Bankruptcy, Settles Long Dispute with Bondholders," *Philadelphia*, September 11, 2015, https://www.phillymag.com/business/2015/09/11/please-touch-museum-bankruptcy/.

42. Jared Shelly, "Hands Off the Please Touch," *Philadelphia*, May 5, 2015, https://www.phillymag.com/news/2015/05/24/hands-off-the-please-touch/.

43. Robin Pogrebin, "The Metropolitan Museum Will Delay a New $600 Million Wing," *New York Times*, January 11, 2017, https://www.nytimes.com/2017/01/11/arts/design/the-metropolitan-museum-will-delay-a-new-600-million-wing.html.

44. Taylor Stevens, " Salt Lake City Serves the Leonardo Museum with Notice of Default over Hundreds of Thousands in Unpaid Debts," *Salt Lake Tribune*, November 27, 2019, https://www.sltrib.com/news/2019/11/26/salt-lake-city-goes-after/.

45. David Wallis, "Start-Up Success Isn't Enough to Found a Museum," *New York Times*, March 9, 2014, https://www.nytimes.com/2014/03/20/arts/artsspecial/start-up-success-isnt-enough-to-found-a-museum.html.

46. Wallis, "Start-Up Success Isn't Enough to Found a Museum."

47. Deb Sopan, "The Newseum Is Increasingly Relevant, but Can It Survive?" *New York Times*, October 22, 2017, https://www.nytimes.com/2017/10/22/arts/design/the-newseum-is-increasingly-relevant-but-can-it-survive.html.

48. Vivian S. Toy, "Museum and Creator Formally Part Ways," *New York Times*, August 8, 2004, https://www.nytimes.com/2004/08/08/nyregion/museum-and-cre ator-formally-part-ways.html.

49. Mike Scutari, "Almost There: Key takeaways from a museum's successful capital campaign," *Inside Philanthropy*, August 6, 2019, https://www.insidephilanthropy.com /home/2019/8/3/the-new-museum-in-new-york-has-announced-details-of-its-63 -million-expansion.

50. "Asian Art Museum Unveils $90 Million Plan to Transform Civic Center Home," Asian Art Museum, September 26, 2017, http://www.asianart.org/press_releases/85.

51. Hilarie M. Sheets, "Norton Museum of Art Opens Grand Expansion," *Art Newspaper*, February 8, 2019, https://www.theartnewspaper.com/news/norton-museum-of-art finds-its-way.

52. Jan Sjostrom, "Palm Beachers Essential to Success of Norton Museum Expansion," *Palm Beach Daily News*, February 3, 2019, https://www.palmbeachdailynews.com /news/20190203/palm-beachers-essential-to-success-of-norton-museum-ex pansion.

53. Stephan Salisbury, "Philadelphia Museum of Art's Record-Breaking Fund-Raising Campaign Passes $455 Million," *Philadelphia Inquirer*, August 7, 2019, https://www .inquirer.com/arts/philadelphia-museum-of-art-capital-campaign-lenfest-diet rich-williams-mcneil-20190807.html.

54. David Wallis, "Start-Up Success Isn't Enough to Found a Museum," *New York Times*, March 9, 2014, https://www.nytimes.com/2014/03/20/arts/artsspecial/start-up -success-isnt-enough-to-found-a-museum.html.

55. Alison Leigh Cowan, "This Time, Rumors of Demise May Be True," *New York Times*, June 3, 2008, https://www.nytimes.com/2008/06/03/nyregion/03twain.html?_r =2&ref=todayspaper&oref=slogin&oref=slogin.

56. "Mark Twain's Home May Close," *NPR WSKG,* June 22, 2008, https://www.npr.org /templates/story/story.php?storyId=91784890.

57. Mary Ellen Godin, "Employee admits embezzling $1 million from Mark Twain House," Reuters, August 5, 2011, https://www.reuters.com/article/us-crime-marktwain -idUSTRE77476H20110805.

58. Alison Leigh Cowan, "This Time, Rumors of Demise May Be True," *New York Times*, June 3, 2008, https://www.nytimes.com/2008/06/03/nyregion/03twain.html?_r =2&ref=todayspaper&oref=slogin&oref=slogin.

59. "990," Mark Twain House, *Guidestar*, accessed February 16, 2020, https://pdf.guide star.org/PDF_Images/2018/060/685/2018-060685118-0fcc45b9-9.pdf.

60. Peter Johnson, "SLO Museum of Art Suspends Plans for New Building Amid Fi- nancial Challenges," *New Times,* January 16, 2020, https://www.newtimesslo.com /sanluisobispo/slo-museum-of-art-suspends-plans-for-new-building-amid-finan cial-challenges/Content?oid=9188948.

61. Tim Elfrink, "Frost Family Bails Out Cash-Strapped Science Museum, Cans Entire Board of Directors," *Miami New Times*, February 10, 2016, https://www.miaminewtimes.com /news/frost-family-bails-out-cash-strapped-science-museum-cans-entire-board -of-directors-8241838.

Chapter 5

6

Taking Care of Business

Sometimes financial matters do not work out despite careful consideration and planning. Many things are simply beyond a museum's control. The financial impact of natural disasters such as Hurricane Katrina, a major downturn in the economy, or a worldwide pandemic rattle a museum's balance sheet. Sudden, adverse financial decisions made by funders or catastrophic infrastructure failures present organizations with major, unexpected financial crises. The timing and magnitude of such events cannot always be predicted, but the challenges must be met nonetheless.

One can argue that some major expenditures, such as catastrophic infrastructure failure, are theoretically within the control of an organization if steps are taken over time to prepare for such an eventuality. Unfortunately, most museums are not in a position to prepare for and put funds aside for every emergency expenditure. Sometimes financial issues are just too big and beyond the means of many organizations. These major issues are not easily addressed. The practical reality is that most museums are focused on short-term challenges, even though they know that a major financial crisis will someday appear. They just hope that it is not in the immediate future.

Even though some funding challenges seem insurmountable, it is still possible to control many financial variables. Much of a museum's financial destiny is within its own grasp, but there must be a willingness to be disciplined and make hard decisions; embrace thoughtful and thorough analysis; take well-considered risks; sacrifice when necessary; and develop and enforce protocols for internal financial controls. These steps are possible for every organization. It is less about money or institutional size than it is about attitude, commitment, and vigilance.

EVERY MUSEUM CAN CONTROL FINANCES

Any museum, large or small, can effectively manage and protect the precious resources under its control. Some museums have fewer resources of staff, but every museum can make finance a top priority. Project expansion activity can be measured and realistic. Thoughtful deliberation and decision-making can be a prime concern. Learning from the experiences of others costs very little. Forecasting realistic revenue projections and monitoring expenditures do not require elaborate systems or staffing. Becoming more entrepreneurial in developing new sources of revenue is possible even with limited resources. Simple preventive measures minimize the possibility of fraud. Financial decisions can be made with reason rather than emotion.

This begins by deciding that financial management is central to the well-being of the museum and deserves adequate time and consideration. It is not just a matter of good record keeping or having a solid understanding of the mechanics of good financial practice. It requires being honest with ourselves, even—especially—if it hurts. Museums must take seriously how they think about, plan, and manage finances and acknowledge that much of it actually *is* within their control. It is too easy to assign blame or shift responsibility for financial failures when issues might have been better controlled in the first place. Museums must do more than just hope things turn out well.

THE OBLIGATIONS OF NONPROFIT FINANCIAL MANAGEMENT

Most museums are nonprofit organizations, which means they exist to benefit the general public. Governance and management are done with the best interests of the public in mind. Nonprofit organizations are not responsible to shareholders but to the public at-large, and profits (if any) are reinvested in the ongoing work of the organization. Because they exist to benefit the public, nonprofit organizations enjoy certain privileges, such as being tax-exempt and providing tax benefits to donors. To maintain that exempt status, trustees must demonstrate that their organization stays true to its mission-related purposes, business is conducted honestly, transparently, and ethically, and its financial and other resources are being used wisely.

Public confidence in the organization and the work it does is critical. Museums must demonstrate that they deserve public support—and this level of trust and confidence must be earned every day. Belief in the organization and its programs is critical to raise funds, as well as attract new trustees, volunteers, and competent staff. Museums and other nonprofits owe their very survival to public perception of the worth of their organizations.

Trustees are fiduciaries for the general public and must work on the public's behalf to look after and manage the interests and resources of the museum. They are held to very high standards and scrutinized by regulatory agencies, funders, and the public at-large because of the high degree of trust conferred upon them. They cannot afford the appearance of conflicts of interest, reckless spending, ill-advised initiatives, impulsive decision-making, or fraudulent activity. The damage can be long-lasting to trustees, management, and the institutions they represent. And because the financial condition of many nonprofits is precarious, even the slightest hint of untoward activity seriously undermines an organization's ability to achieve its purposes or even survive.

One of a trustee's most important responsibilities is finance. Jennifer Rottmann, in her work on policies and procedures for nonprofits, summarizes why financial management in nonprofits is so critical. She writes that it has far-reaching effects with both internal and external ramifications, including: 1) being essential for efficiency in operation and delivery of mission services; 2) safeguarding assets from fraud; 3) complying with regulatory rules; 4) being transparent and accountable to the public; and 5) having the ability to make good, informed decisions.[1]

Because managing a museum's finances ultimately rests squarely on the shoulders of trustees, they are charged with taking financial matters seriously. Protecting and managing the assets of the organization are among the most important of their many responsibilities. In fact, the "Duty of Care" is arguably the most important of a trustee's legal obligations. Defined as the judgment and decision-making "an ordinarily prudent person in a like position would use in similar circumstances," Duty of Care simply means that trustees are expected to take great care in the management of finances and other responsibilities entrusted to them.[2]

In practical terms, this means that trustees will make informed judgments for the organizations in which they serve. They are obligated to secure and assess information; review and analyze reports; ask questions; seek independent, outside perspectives; and generally avoid casual, capricious decision-making.[3] In order to do this, trustees must exercise sound financial oversight and recordkeeping; comply with governmental regulations and reports; manage against fraud; engage in prudent risk-taking and investment activity; protect against potential insolvency; and ensure the survival of the organization. This must be taken seriously and is among a trustee's most important duties, but it takes time and commitment. It does not require elaborate systems and staff resources as much as institutional attention.

FINANCIAL SYSTEMS AND FINANCIAL JUDGMENT

Many financial responsibilities are relatively straightforward because the fundamentals of financial reporting are structured with prescribed ways of presenting information. The Financial Accounting Standards Board recommends that nonprofits conform to Generally Accepted Accounting Principles (GAAP) so that nonprofits present their financials records and reports in standardized fashion to allow outside parties to more easily understand an organization's financial reporting and discern its level of transparency.[4]

Without the standardization of GAAP, it is very difficult for accrediting bodies, regulators, grantors, donors, auditors, and lenders— even the professional staff—to clearly understand an organization's finances and compare those against past performance and that of other organizations. It is also helpful for those trustees who may already be accustomed to GAAP compliant documents in their for-profit enterprises. Being GAAP compliant creates a high level of confidence in the accuracy and consistency of financial reporting, and many external agencies even require GAAP-compliant reports.[5]

The Internal Revenue Service (IRS) requires most nonprofit exempt organizations to file IRS Form 990, an annual standardized report designed to provide extensive information about a nonprofit organization's activities.[6] The "990" takes a comprehensive look at the overall financial and programmatic picture of nonprofits and includes detailed information on assets and liabilities; operating income and expenditures; fundraising; program service accomplishments; governance; executive compensation; investments; conflicts of interest; and much more.[7]

The presentation of basic information in these reports is probably somewhat familiar to many trustees from their respective work experiences, even if they come from the for-profit world. It is therefore reasonable to assume that these trustees have a reasonable understanding of financial reports and can navigate these areas with relatively little support. Mostly, it just takes a little time and effort.

Scrupulous analysis and understanding of the "numbers" and balancing the budget are critical, of course, but these alone do not guarantee prudent financial decision-making. Trustees' financial responsibilities extend well beyond just keeping track of expenditures, understanding financial statements, and protecting an organization's assets. Financial information must also be used as an effective tool for improving performance, developing policy, and making the most informed decisions possible. Coupled with a museum's mission, they form the very basis of all museum decision-making, and a blend of each is required. Financial considerations alone may short-circuit important mission-driven activities, and mission considerations absent financial realities may result in reckless spending. The question must always be this: How will our organization use financial reports to effectively manage the museumand its mission?

William P. Ryan, writing in the *Nonprofit Quarterly*, gives some excellent advice for how financial record keeping, internal controls, and judgment work together to make financial management a key tool for the overall management of a nonprofit organization. He notes three important areas:

USING JUDGMENT AND SYSTEMS TO PREVENT MALFEASANCE

Ryan believes that a trustee's first financial responsibility is to prevent malfeasance, which he states requires both the systems to manage finance and the judgment to question and effectively use the information found within them. He emphasizes that using only one of these tools is inadequate. An organization must have strong financial systems, of course—"with reg- ular, thorough financial reports and sound controls"—which provide the essential information for protecting the assets of the organization. Ryan goes on to say, however, that the reports and controls must be coupled with "judgment and vigilance"—trustees must carefully read reports, question those things they don't understand, or express concern for financial con- trols that are ineffective. He believes that most nonprofit financial scandals happen in organizations that have systems in place, but trustees often are not willing to question the reports or participate in discussions. On the other hand, relying solely on the board to detect financial problems without having adequate systems in place is pointless because discerning untoward activity is difficult if no systems are there to help discover irregularities.

MOVING FINANCIAL INFORMATION FROM THE BACK OFFICE TO THE BOARDROOM

Ryan believes it is essential for boards to integrate financial information into its decision-making if it is to do more than just protect its resources. Protecting resources is important, but supporting and advancing the or- ganization's mission is paramount. He believes that financial information must be used to help shape an organization's strategy or even the mission itself. It should not be relegated to the "back office," just for the use of bookkeepers. Many issues and initiatives are difficult to discuss and their implications not fully understood without full use of financial information.

REMEMBERING THAT MONEY ISN'T EVERYTHING

Lastly, Ryan reminds us that money isn't everything. He fears that boards sometimes focus only on finances for decision-making because finance offers such a level of clarity. The danger here, of course, is that relying on financial information alone provides a gross simplification and a one-sided perspective. Consequently, he writes, if organizations rely too much on finance to make decisions, they will pay less attention to other aspects of performance, such as programming and services. He also notes that financial reporting is retrospective—it tells us how we did in previous months or years—but it doesn't tell us why we did well or poorly or how we might improve to meet the needs of our constituencies. Balancing the budget doesn't necessarily mean that an institution had a successful year in providing services or that it was responsive to the community. He believes there is a danger in overusing financial information as much as there is a danger in underusing it.

Balancing a budget is easy if an institution is only concerned about the bottom line. It is much more difficult if it is equally concerned about its mission. The mission of a nonprofit is not to balance the budget, but to provide services to the public. Responsible financial management, however, is an important means to that end.[8]

TAKING CHARGE OF FINANCES

One of the fundamental steps in managing an organization's finances is to have in place approved policies and controls that prescribe protocols for conducting financial business. Every organization must have such protocols if trustees are to fulfill their fiduciary responsibilities. Policies and internal controls mandate what the board feels is important to satisfactorily manage institutional responsibilities for finance. They provide the context, parameters, and procedures for how the museum conducts its financial life. Among other things, policies and controls include considerations such as handling and recording assets; segregating duties; limiting authority; controlling investment activity; managing contracts and purchasing procedures; and defining reporting requirements. In addition, policies and controls clarify the roles, authority, and responsibilities of those involved in financial management and decision-making.

There is a distinction between policy and internal controls, with the former being more prescriptive and the latter more procedural. Elizabeth H. Foley writes that the difference between policies and internal controls is that policies should be thought of as *overall intent* and internal controls should be thought of as the *specific mechanics* to carry out the intent.[9]

The size of the budget is irrelevant in managing finances. Every organization can and should define how it will conduct its financial affairs. In the absence of adopted policies and procedures, staff and board members are likely to operate under a set of assumptions that may or may not be accurate or productive; consequently, the organization experiences financial chaos.

WHAT HAPPENS WITHOUT POLICIES AND CONTROLS

Policies and controls help protect the assets of the organization; create reliable and accurate financial reporting; promote compliance with laws and regulations; help facilitate more effective and efficient operations; reduce the likelihood of fraud, mismanagement, or error; and force more accountability and consistency. Lack of sufficient policies and internal controls, or lack of enforcement if they already exist, is often the cause of many financial problems. Unfortunately, it often takes a crime or a major decision gone wrong to recognize the importance of financial protocols.

Over a five-year period, the chief deputy director of a major West Coast museum, aided by the museum's chief accountant and a museum secretary, embezzled approximately $2.1 million, spending lavishly on cars, jewelry, personal debts, and tax obligations. According to the deputy district attorney, the museum had "only one person looking over the purse strings, a person in whom they [museum officials] had extreme confidence. He had control over the books and no one was looking over his shoulder. And that's a perfect recipe for theft."[10]

In 2015, the treasurer of an historical organization in Connecticut was arrested on embezzlement charges when it was discovered that he made $20,100 in unauthorized withdrawals from the organization's accounts. The treasurer was the only person who had access to the account, and when confronted, he told the board that he withdrew the money and deposited it into his personal account to "get a better return on the money" for the museum. In fact, at no time did he reinvest the money and instead spent the money on personal purchases.[11]

The former director of a Montana museum admitted taking $30,941 over a four-year period and pleaded guilty to felony theft of taking cash from museum receipts, donations, gift shop sales, and funds given to him for the museum by a tour company. The theft was discovered when the director became ill and the trustees began directly managing museum affairs. Until that time, the director was the only person with access to museum finances. Some of the funds were allegedly used to subsidize the director's side business of making saddles.[12]

These are examples of organizations that did not have or did not enforce basic policies and procedures for counting and handling cash, reconciling bank statements, moving money to different accounts without authorization, and conducting investment activity without approval. Often only one individual had total control over finances. Financial control mechanisms were centered around the trust placed in these individuals without regard for systems and oversight that quickly recognize irregularities. The good news is that simple oversight likely would have recognized financial improprieties before significant damage was done.

In another case, a museum was the victim of an embezzlement scheme when its finance director stole approximately $200,000 over a three-year period. An audit was ordered when trustees began to have concerns about the organization's finances. The results of the audit pointed to questionable dealings by the finance director, much to the surprise of the trustees. The need for trust *and* systems was "very much a learning curve for us," said the executive director, and new practices were soon put in place to guard against future wrongdoing. Fortunately, the losses were not crippling for the museum, but once again, such an incident likely would not have occurred had simple oversight procedures been in place.[13]

An employee at a Chicago museum was accused of embezzling $903,000 by keeping cash payments for memberships and stealing cash from patron drink tickets at membership events. The defense attorney asserted that the amount was actually closer to $410,000, and other employees, not his client, could have taken the remainder of the money because the "system in place would make it easy for others to do it." The museum recovered all but $10,000 of its losses from insurance and subsequently instituted much stricter oversight over its cash-handling procedures.[14]

In a unique case in Washington, a museum violated its own policies when its executive director withdrew at least $100,000 from the museum's endowment and transferred the funds to her own account. Museum policy specified that two board members must sign off on any withdrawal from the endowment. In less than three years, approximately $460,000 was transferred to her personal bank account and used for personal purposes with numerous unauthorized checks written to her in excess of her salary. As a result of this breach in policy, museum membership voted out all incumbent executive board members. In this case, the policy was in place but not enforced. It is an important reminder that in all policy matters and internal control procedures, it is not enough just to mandate certain systems—they must also be enforced.[15]

Specific policies and procedures vary widely depending on the organization's budget size, staffing, and operations. There is no "one size fits all" template that works for all organizations. Smaller organizations with few or no staff have needs and policies that are far different and less complex than those of larger institutions. The important thing is that systems exist to guide financial record keeping, decision-making, and oversight; otherwise, there will be chaos and no accountability. In a field that is so focused on its finances, having too few policies or controls is dangerous and prevents an organization from managing scarce resources effectively.[16]

An excellent example of policies and controls that were proactively instituted to define the limits of allowable financial activity was the policy

Shelburne Museum developed in 1996 to define how a newly established $25 million endowment was to be managed. The endowment, known as the Collections Care Endowment, was created from the proceeds of a controversial sale of twenty-two paintings and sculptures from the museum's collections.[17] Instead of using proceeds to purchase new objects for the collections, the museum determined that the funds would be more prudently spent by creating an endowment specifically for the care of the museum's vast collections. The need to carefully manage how the funds would be spent became especially important not only to guide the program, but also to make clear its true intent given the intense level of scrutiny that it received.

The Collections Care Endowment policies began with a definition of what constituted collections care as defined by the museum. The definition was written to include three main areas: 1) Preventive and Corrective Conservation; 2) Curatorial Activity; and 3) Protection. The policies went into more detail, mandating that the funds be segregated and separately managed and there would be no invasion of principal; the approved income draw would be 4.5 percent or less; a detailed plan for use of income would be presented for trustee approval annually and a super-majority vote of trustees would be required for any policy changes regarding the Collections Care Endowment.

The detailed policy was ultimately approved and provided the guidance necessary to effectively and responsibly manage the proceeds of the sale. It also assisted the staff and board in decision-making and at the same time created a level of confidence in constituencies who felt that the museum might spend the funds inappropriately if no guidelines were in place.[18]

POLICY

Financial management begins with the development of financial policy, defined as the "high level overall plan embracing the general goals" of an organization in order to "guide and determine present and future decisions," as well as demonstrate "prudence or wisdom in the management of affairs."[19] Policies are essentially the big-picture rules or principles of an organization that form the basis for what is considered important by the organization. Policies provide the broad guidance and philosophy from which the board and staff work to conduct the museum's financial life, or as Foley reminds us, an organization's "intent."[20]

Policies provide a reference point for identifying and managing conflicts and defining appropriate action and ethical conduct. Development and approval of policies is one of the board's most important responsibilities because they define the limits of authority delegated to staff and the role of the board in financial oversight and decision-making.[21] They also protect the staff and board (assuming the policies are enforced) because they clarify appropriate conduct and mandate transparency in financial matters.

While the board articulates and oversees "intent," compliance with its policies and the execution of the policy is most often handled by the staff under the supervision of the CEO. The CEO manages and enforces the policy on a daily basis. There may be board-approved policies for budget approval; spending limits; CEO authority to authorize expenditures; real estate acquisition; conflict of interest; compensation; and more depending on the needs of the particular organization. It is essential that museums have clear and overarching policies *in writing* to provide guidance that is consistent and board approved. Policies may be updated from time to time and change in response to the changing needs of an institution. They are considered to be of such importance that they require full board deliberation and approval.

Certain organizational documents are required of nonprofits to be in compliance with various regulations and laws governing nonprofits. These are not really considered policies as such, but they are necessary to obtain and keep an organization's nonprofit status. These documents include such things as articles of incorporation, mission statement, and bylaws. Bylaws are particularly important for finance because they usually include guidance about financial matters such as limits of authority; role of the Treasurer; authority to enter into contracts; management of assets; audit requirements; and more.

In order to maintain public trust, it is important that organizations manage themselves according to the most effective, transparent, and accountable best practices in the execution of their financial responsibilities The Internal Revenue Service recommends that nonprofits have certain governance policies in place, although they are not required because corporate nonprofit law is governed by the states; however, IRS Form 990 does ask a series of questions about whether an organization has certain approved policies in place. Those without basic policies are likely to raise red flags in the eyes of the public, funders, and regulators and stand a greater chance of being audited.[22]

Further emphasizing nonprofit accountability was the 2002 Sarbanes-Oxley Act, also known as the "American Competitiveness and Accountability Act."[23] Sarbanes-Oxley was designed in response to major corporate scandals and fraudulent accounting practices (such as Enron and World-Com). It was designed to rebuild confidence in the corporate sector, ensure more accountability and adequate internal financial controls, and improve oversight. Most provisions relate to public companies, and the law was not aimed at nonprofits, although at least two provisions in particular relate to nonprofits. The law prohibits 1) Retaliation against whistleblowers and 2) Destruction of financial records that could be used in an official investigation. While only these two provisions applied to nonprofits, it did suggest that nonprofit board services should be taken seriously and ultimately "did effect a positive change of context and behavior for nonprofits in the areas of governance and financial accountability."[24]

Below are some common, but by no means definitive, policies directly related to museum finance. If trustees desire more control over financial matters, they are likely to have even more policies to guide the CEO and staff. While the nature and extent of policies may vary from institution to institution, the following are key policies for every organization. It is important to note that policies must be approved *and* enforced; otherwise, they are meaningless.

GENERAL FINANCIAL

General financial policies may be numerous depending on the needs and complexity of each museum's operation. They may include broader, intent-based policies, or they may be more focused and relatively detailed, although not to the point of being a specific, step-by-step procedural document. Most organizations choose general, all-encompassing financial policies that lay out the institutional philosophy and approach, but they leave the operational details to a comprehensive articulation of internal controls. Because financial issues are so far-reaching and have many components, there are likely to be many general financial policies that outline the scope, limits, and authority of financial authority and level of oversight. Because of the size, range, and complexity of museums, there is no template that works for everyone, but some of the most common policies include authority to sign contracts; limits to authorize expenditures; authority to engage in contracts, loans, and other financial commitments; fixed assets; investments; audits; and segregation of duties. Once again, it is important to remember that policies must be monitored and enforced on a regular basis.

CONFLICTS OF INTEREST

This is one policy that is important for all nonprofits. Because museum staff and trustees work on behalf of the general public, it is important that they put that responsibility above any personal interest or financial gain. A conflict of interest may exist when a board member, employee, or volunteer has competing interests or loyalties. They should make the best interests of the museum paramount at all times, and the public should have complete confidence in museum leadership to make decisions that are in the best interests of the museum. This is called the "Duty of Loyalty" and means that board or staff service should not be used, or perceived as being used, for personal gain. For example, it may be in an individual trustee's best interest if the museum contracted with that trustee's law firm to conduct the museum's legal affairs. This, however, could raise issues of trustees enriching themselves at the museum's expense. On the other hand, if the trustee law firm specialized in nonprofit law and offered the museum a generously reduced hourly or even pro-bono rate, a case could be made that the arrangement was actually made in the best interests of the museum. The important thing is that the competing interests are revealed and there is a prescribed method of resolving the conflict. It must also take into consideration the *appearance* of a conflict, which may be just as bad as an actual conflict.

An excellent example of a conflict-of-interest issue was when a major historical organization purchased a parcel of land from the former mayor of the city in which the organization was located. The mayor, who also was a museum board member when talks began regarding the purchase of the property, reputedly had personal and political connections to the historical organization's director. The property was sold to the historical organization by the former mayor for a price considerably above the market rate for such a property at the time. The property was also sold without the customary real estate appraisal. This transaction, along with other questionable dealings at the organization, resulted in scandalous news articles that accused the former mayor/trustee and the organization's director of colluding to enrich themselves. Eventually, the director resigned his position, and considerable harm was done to the reputation of the organization.[25]

The board must use its judgment in determining whether there is a true conflict and what, if anything, needs to be done. One of the key issues is that even if there is no conflict and an arrangement ultimately benefits the museum, the public may perceive a conflict of interest, which affects public perception of trustee motivation in decision-making and the reputation of the institution.[26]

WHISTLEBLOWERS

Whistleblower protection is mandated by law in Sarbanes-Oxley, but an institutional whistleblower policy is not; however, it is advisable to take proactive steps to let employees, volunteers, and the public know that reporting suspected wrongdoing is encouraged without fear of retaliation.[27] Such a policy protects an employee for reporting misconduct in the workplace. The employee cannot be subject to retaliatory actions such as firing, demotion, harassment, or other inappropriate responses.

Examples of things in the museum workplace that a whistleblower might reveal may include such things as improper expenditures; inappropriate use of assets; theft; unauthorized destruction of records; violation of conflict-of-interest policies; harassment; or any other activity that violates museum policy or lawful conduct. The Whistleblower policy encourages staff and volunteers to be forthcoming with information without fear of retaliation and gives the trustees an opportunity to learn of inappropriate or illegal conduct.

Protecting the "whistleblower" helps prevent financial fraud and wrong-doing that might be caught at an early stage. Policies usually include a written process in which an employee identifies wrongdoing and the employer deals with the complaint through a systematic investigation and resolution. Finally, putting a procedure in place for employees to raise and address problems is healthy for the organization while alleviating any concerns over retaliation to the reporting employee.[28]

CODE OF ETHICS

A code of ethics is a formalized statement of an organization's beliefs and values for how it conducts business. It is an essential part of an organization's culture. It helps guide principles of conduct and behavior in the workplace and articulates what the organization feels is important in the way it does business. Generally, all persons associated with an organization—volunteers, staff, and trustees—are expected to read, commit to, and sign a code-of-ethics statement. The code of ethics goes beyond simply complying with laws and regulations that are required of everyone. A code of ethics articulates a higher standard of behavior, which is particularly important for museums that must put themselves beyond reproach in their public-trust responsibilities.[29]

As an example, the Association of Art Museum Directors (AAMD) sanctioned one museum for what it considered ethical violations when the museum sold artwork to fund various endowment and expansion programs rather than support collections activity.[30] The AAMD requested its 243 member organizations not lend to the museum or collaborate with it on exhibition programs, saying that, "Selling art to support any need other than to build a museum's collection fundamentally undermines the critically important relationships between museums, donors and the public," and "when museums violate the trust of their donors and the public, they diminish the opportunity and responsibility to make great works of art available to the public."[31]

Nonprofit members of the American Alliance of Museums (AAM) are expected to comply with its Code of Ethics for Museums, which states in part, "Museums in the United States are grounded in the tradition of public service. . . . Members of their governing authority, employees and volunteers are committed to the interests of these beneficiaries . . . Museums and those responsible for them must do more than avoid legal liability; they must take affirmative steps to maintain their integrity so as to warrant public confidence."[32]

DOCUMENT RETENTION AND DISPOSAL

The other criminal provision mandated by the Sarbanes-Oxley Act is for organizations to have a formal records retention and destruction policy for financial and other records. It also prohibits the destruction of documents that may be relevant to a federal investigation. Sarbanes-Oxley makes it a crime to knowingly and "corruptly" conceal, alter, destroy, or make false entries in any document, with the intent to impede or obstruct the investigation of an official proceeding or potential crime, within the jurisdiction of the federal government.[33] IRS Form 990 asks whether an organization has a retention and disposal policy, and most organizations are adopting them.

There are some key organizational documents that have state or federal requirements for retention. These include key corporate documents such as Articles of Incorporation, IRS Determination letter (which grants nonprofit status), organizational bylaws, and tax returns. These documents should be kept permanently (with all approved revisions to bylaws). Other records, such as audits, bank statements, donor and grant records, and employment files, are records that should be kept and placed on a document retention and disposal schedule where appropriate. Permanently keeping board minutes, the official proceedings of an organization, is also essential.

It is a good idea to consult with auditors on retention schedules for certain types of documents. It is also important to make certain an organization is complying with state and federal requirements for retaining documents. State and federal laws list records retention as a requirement for receiving grants. As a general rule, nonprofits should keep all documents for at least three years, and much longer—even permanently—in other cases.

Retention and disposal policies should specify the time period for the retention of certain documents, the manner in which they will be stored, and the means of disposal. Not only will document-retention schedules help protect an organization against legal action and any questions of institutional transparency, but it will also provide a means of reducing costs of accumulated-document storage and related management costs.

During the real estate financial scandal previously noted, the situation was made much worse and the public perception dampened even more when there were allegations that the museum had shredded and removed documents, allegedly impeding the investigation.[34]

HUMAN RESOURCES

Nonprofits must comply with all local, state, and federal employment laws in hiring and terminating employees. There are many areas of the law that require compliance and have significant financial implications. These include discrimination; equal opportunity; sexual harassment; safe working environments; workers compensation; and whistleblower policies, among others.

In addition to the areas prescribed by law, organizations may have policies of their own. These may include hiring practices; termination procedures; performance evaluations; compensation schedules; training opportunities; equipment usage; vacation and sick leave; work hours; compensatory time; insurance; and dress codes; to name just a few.

It is important to carefully document an organization's human resource procedures and practices because certain areas are particularly vulnerable to legal action. Organizations must document that they have complied with such important laws as the Americans with Disabilities Act, Title VII of the Civil Rights Act, the Family Medical Leave Act, and the Age Discrimination Act, among others. In addition, organizations must have documentation that demonstrates their compliance with their own institutional policies. Major areas of lawsuits relate to discrimination; wrongful termination; harassment; workplace injury; and wage violations. Nearly all human-relations policies have significant financial implications.

Often such actions are settled out of court as an efficient, less public, and comparatively inexpensive way of addressing an issue—even when the museum has overwhelming documentation supporting its case. As an example, one museum was threatened with a lawsuit because it did not hire a minority-owned business for contracted services, the owner claiming he was discriminated against because of his race. In fact, he did not get the job because his proposal did not address the required qualifications and his business did not have the required resources of other more competitive proposals. Over a year was spent by the museum assembling documentation demonstrating that the process was fair; in fact, the museum had an excellent record of nondiscrimination in its practices. Nonetheless, the museum's insurer wished to minimize their financial exposure and decided to pay out the sum of $40,000 to the claimant rather than engage in a protracted lawsuit—which the insurance company indicated the museum would easily win but would cost the insurer much more—perhaps as much as several hundred thousand dollars.[35] In addition, a lawsuit would create negative public relations implications for the museum even if it won the case.

Naturally there are legitimate cases brought against museums for discrimination and other reasons, but without documentation it becomes difficult for a museum to counter such claims and defend itself. Unfortunately, while having thorough documentation may win the legal case, it may not always win the public relations case. Nonetheless, museums must be as scrupulous as possible with employee record keeping and documentation—and always remember that museum administrators must never violate the museum's own policies.

Finally, it is important that human resource policies and their procedures for employees and volunteers must always be reviewed by an attorney, approved by the full board, and presented in clear and concise writing, usually in the form of a human resource policy manual. Policies should be given to every employee and volunteer with written acknowledgment that the document was received.[36]

CONFIDENTIALITY

It is important that trustees and leadership understand the critical nature of confidentiality to a nonprofit organization. Having a policy underscores and articulates its importance. Because trustees and museum leadership have access to considerable information that is sensitive, such information must be discussed discreetly. Certain information learned or used in decisions must not be fully divulged without proper authorization. Since so much of a nonprofit management is built around trust with its constituencies, violation of that trust or exposure of confidential information can be disastrous. Usually this happens for three main reasons: 1) Disclosure of confidential information discussed during a board meeting when participants disclose sensitive information about strategy, political matters, contract negotiations, donor solicitation plans, or job performance; 2) disclosure of personal information such as illness, legal matters, or family crises that may be relevant for board discussion but not public consumption; and 3) conflicts of interest, when members share confidential discussions from board meetings with outside parties or when trustees use information from board meetings for personal financial advantage.[37]

As an example, a newly hired museum director in transit to his new job received a phone call from senior staff who alerted the new director that an office staff member who had access to confidential information was distributing the terms of the new director's contract to the staff. Since the contract allowed for many provisions that were well beyond those of the regular staff, the news caused considerable resentment of the new director and created unnecessary challenges even before he started his new job. It also called into question the staff member's trustworthiness on all other confidential museum business to which she had access.

Nonprofit board meetings in some cases are open to the public, but confidential matters must be discussed in executive sessions, when only trustees and necessary guests are allowed to participate. Members of the public must be asked to leave to avoid unnecessary embarrassment or violation of trust between the museum and its constituencies. In general, matters relating to legal issues, personnel discussions, or the potential sale or purchase of real estate are reserved for executive sessions.[38] Information that is confidential, privileged, or proprietary should not be discussed without authorization, and great care should be taken to ensure that such information is not inadvertently shared with unauthorized individuals. Anyone divulging such information must be disciplined, which may include dismissal.[39]

The protection of privacy is a fundamental tenet of good organizational ethics, and for nonprofit organizations a confidentiality policy is essential because so much reliance is placed on public trust and relationships. As an example, the Association of Fundraising Professionals, in its Code of Ethical Standards, states that members will "protect the confidentiality of all privileged information relating to the provider/client relationships."[40] Think about the potential damage if a staff member released confidential personal and financial information from the museum's donor files. It is fair to say that the museum's relationship with those donors would be over.

COMPENSATION

IRS Form 990 asks organizations for information about how they determine compensation for officers and key employees: "Did the process for determining compensation of the following persons include a review and approval by independent persons, comparability data, and contemporaneous substantiation of the deliberation and decision?"[41] Then it asks that the procedures for determining compensation be described.

Designed to make nonprofit finance more transparent, IRS Form 990 asks governing bodies to look at comparable salaries of individuals at similar organizations with similar responsibilities and use this as a basis for determining compensation. It also asks whether the process for determining reasonable compensation has been put in writing contemporaneously with compensation decisions. If it is determined that an individual is being overpaid, the person must repay the overpayment to the organization in addition to paying an excise tax to the IRS equal to 25 percent of the overpayment. Those participating in the overpayment, who are aware that it is an excess benefit, are also subject to a tax equal to 10 percent of the excess up to a maximum of $20,000.

Nonprofit organizations need to pay particular attention to all perquisites (or "perks") and treat them as part of total compensation, and be sure that the total compensation does not exceed what is reasonable.[42]

INVESTMENT AND SPENDING POLICY

Trustees of museums have a fiduciary responsibility to protect and grow the assets of their organization and make certain the assets are used to further the mission of the institution. One of the ways organizations do this is to place some of their financial resources in various types of investments, most often in an institutional endowment.

Naturally, investing brings with it a certain element of risk. The investment approach must be prudent and well-considered and the level of risk tolerance well-defined and comfortable for the organization. Before investing, an organization must develop an Investment Policy to help it articulate its overall philosophy, define specific objectives, and monitor its investment activities. Investment policies vary widely between organizations because every organization has different needs or approaches to protect the value of its assets, grow the assets to increase long-term value, or desire more access to assets for cash needs for operations or emergencies. Some organizations rely more heavily on short-term cash needs to help fund operational needs, while others may have less short-term cash needs and may wish to focus on longer-term growth.

Usually, the board assigns day-to-day responsibility for investments to an outside fund management firm while the board retains overall responsibility for investment performance. To mitigate such risks, many nonprofits consider the need to diversify their investments and hire professional investment managers to monitor market values, provide advice, and carry out the actual trades of investments.[43]

Investment policies typically contain information regarding responsibility for investing: long-term goals; risk tolerance; time horizons; a spending policy that defines how much will be spent on a yearly basis; asset class guidelines that define the types and percentages of investment placed in each class; performance goals; guidelines for rebalancing asset class allocations; prohibited transactions or philosophy on socially responsible investing; duties of the investment manager; criteria and qualifications and selection of the investment manager; and expectations and frequency for performance reports.

Spending policy is conducted in harmony with the Investment Policy. Spending policy refers to how assets from investments are spent in the short-term while maintaining a critical balance with longer-term objectives for growth—e.g., too much short-term spending from investment income has a negative impact on the ability of investments to grow over time. The Spending Policy articulates formulas and limits for spending and creates discipline and predictability in income. The most common approach is called "Total Return," which essentially employs a rolling average market value over a period of years (usually three to five years). Then it bases income on a designated percentage of that rolling average. By averaging the market value of several years and taking a percentage (often 5 percent, but sometimes more depending on cash needs), the museum evens out annual income from the endowment and avoids extreme changes from year to year. This approach is more predictable and allows for more accurate operational planning.[44]

GIFT ACCEPTANCE POLICY

Museums actively pursue financial and other gifts to support their needs. Yet sometimes it makes more sense for an institution to actually decline a gift when accepting the gift creates undue complications or financial hardships—the gift may actually cost the organization more to accept! The true benefit of gifts must be carefully analyzed because they may come with too many restrictions, or the nature of the gift is simply not a priority. Certain types of gifts may consume critical storage space, require considerable maintenance, or simply add more work to an already overworked staff. Also, it is important to consider whether the gift runs counter to the museum's values, whether there are complicated legal issues involved in accepting the gift, and whether the museum has the resources and staff to use and maintain the item or even dispose of and liquidate the item entirely. The same is true of accepting art and artifact collections that are not always consistent with collections goals, but museum leadership feels there is a political obligation or financial incentive to accept the gift.

Maryland Nonprofits suggests that Gift Acceptance Policies should articulate the types of gifts or property that will be accepted; the purposes for which they will be accepted; limitation of entities from which the organization will receive gifts; and whether certain unusual gifts will be accepted given the organizational mission and capacity to do so.[45]

INTERNAL CONTROLS

Internal controls are the more specific financial nuts-and-bolts systems that implement board financial policies. These prescribe specific procedures for such things as spending limits; expenditure approvals; record keeping; purchase orders; credit card usage; and many others. Without a consistent way to manage the complexity of finances on a day-to-day basis, there will likely be indiscriminate spending, haphazard record keeping, and no accountability. Lack of controls also makes it easier to commit fraud because it is more difficult to discern whether something was authorized or recorded. Usually the staff, through the CEO, manages internal controls. It is critical that the internal controls are followed without exception by everyone; otherwise, they are useless.[46]

In one instance, a major museum prescribed rules for staff use of museum credit cards, procedures for reimbursing the museum if personal charges were made, and how expenses were to be coded. Over a period of time, the museum director made significant personal charges to the museum's credit card, but did not reimburse the museum promptly or otherwise make arrangements for payment of the debt—despite repeated billings by the finance department. It finally took board intervention for the director to repay charges that totaled over $40,000!

Successful internal controls do a number of things. They reduce the likelihood of losing assets by fraud or error, increase the efficiency of operations, and make financial reporting more reliable. They also reduce the cost of audits and ensure compliance with applicable laws and regulations. It is important to remember that these systems do not guarantee problem-free financial management. They can only provide *reasonable assurances* and minimize the possibility of errors or wrongdoing. There will always be mistakes, bad judgments, management overrides to prescribed procedures, and deliberate fraud even when controls are in place.

Because the needs of every museum are different, there is no "one size fits all" system of internal controls. Internal control procedures can be as extensive and detailed as the institution deems appropriate, although if the goal is compliance, the simpler the procedures, the better. Some of the areas that might be included are procedures for cash disbursements; cash receipts and petty cash; accounts receivable and accounts payables; reimbursements; and check requests. Controls may also include procedures for travel advances; grants accounting; payroll; financial reporting and budgeting; check signing authority; and use of credit cards. In general, the most effective internal controls are those that have a strong segregation of duties—e.g., the person writing the checks should not be the same person signing the checks. The more persons involved in financial processes, the lower the likelihood of error or falsification.

It is essential to create an internal controls manual that details in writing procedures to be followed. This enables all involved to understand their roles and provides a consistent way of maintaining systems regardless of a change in personnel.[47]

A NOTE ABOUT FRAUD

Museums are not institutions where "mega-fraud" is perpetrated on a level such as the embezzlement activities of financiers Robert Vesco and Bernie Madoff, simply because such massive sums of money are generally not there.[48] And even for the wealthier institutions, large sums would be more difficult to hide. Fraud in museums is still impactful, however, whether it is stealing cash receipts from the local county historical museum or perpetrating major frauds against larger museums.

In a 2020 study of 2,504 for-profit and nonprofit organizations, the Association of Certified Fraud Examiners estimated that organizations lose about 5 percent of their revenue to fraud each year. In nonprofits, the median loss was $75,000, with an average loss of $639,000. Most are perpetrated as a result of three main weaknesses: 1) lack of internal controls 2) lack of management review and 3) override of existing controls.[49]

SUMMARY

The lack of systematic procedures, guiding policies, and proper checks and balances may create serious financial problems, even chaos. This makes decision-making more difficult because record keeping may not be consistent or accurate; controls over who has spending authority and how much they can spend is not articulated; careful cash management is not practiced; and spending and revenue projections amount to little more than speculation. And sometimes policies and procedures exist, but they are not uniformly practiced by everyone. Sometimes no one is watching. This leads to a greater likelihood of fraud—theft, misappropriation of funds, forgery, and other untoward activity. And this does even account for theft of those resources that are not directly financial in nature— equipment, materials, and supplies . . . even collections themselves, which are also vulnerable to fraud.

Museums can control how they manage finances, and it begins with an acknowledgment that finances are important and must be treated as a priority. It is about paying attention and exercising responsible oversight. And it is about instituting a solid system of financial policies and internal controls to "watch the store." While not foolproof, they will go a long way in helping manage resources, minimize fraud, make better decisions, and plan effectively for the future.

ORGANIZATIONS THAT ENJOY SUCCESS:

Know that regular, conscientious oversight and attention are key.
Take seriously the roles and responsibilities of those involved in financial oversight and management.

Create policies and controls to address how finances are to be managed and enforce them.

Recognize they cannot control every mistake or transgression, but design systems to minimize the possibility.

Make clear the roles, responsibilities, and authority in financial management.

Create policies and internal controls that fit their needs and make them simple and easy to understand.

Treat financial reports and documentation as an important part of the decision-making process.

NOTES

1. Jennifer Rottmann, "Financial Policies and Procedures Manuals for Nonprofit Organizations: Applying Best Practices to the Environmental Health Strategy Center" (PhD diss., University of Southern Maine, 2011), https://digitalcommons.usm.maine.edu/cgi/viewcontent.cgi?referer=&httpsredir=1&article=1051&context=muskie_capstones.
2. Gene Takagi, "Duty of Care," Nonprofit Law Blog, May 14, 2006, http://nonprofitlawblog.com/duty_of_care/.
3. Jeremy Barlow, "Nonprofit Board Legal Responsibilities," Board Effect, August 12, 2016, https://www.boardeffect.com/blog/non-profit-board-legal-responsibilities/.
4. Shawn H. Miller, "Generally Accepted Accounting Principles," Nonprofit Accounting Basics, January 02, 2019, https://www.nonprofitaccountingbasics.org/accounting-bookkeeping/generally-accepted-accounting-principles.
5. "GAAP and Not-for-profits," Financial Accounting Foundation, accessed July 28, 2020, https://www.accountingfoundation.org/jsp/Foundation/Page/FAFBridgePage&cid=1176164540119.
6. "Annual Filing and Forms," IRS, https://www.irs.gov/charities-non-profits/annual-filing-and-forms.
7. "Form 990," IRS, accessed July 28, 2020, https://www.irs.gov/pub/irs-pdf/f990.pdf.
8. William P. Ryan, "Financial Responsibility of Boards," *NonProfit Quarterly*, March 21, 2001, https://nonprofitquarterly.org/financial-responsibility-of-boards/.
9. "Reporting and Operations," *Nonprofit Accounting Basics*, https://www.nonprofitaccountingbasics.org/reporting-operations/policies.
10. John M. Glionna, "3 Charged in Embezzlement at L.A. Museum," *Los Angeles Times*, July 13, 1995, https://www.latimes.com/archives/la-xpm-1995-07-13-mn-23539-story.html.
11. David Moran, "Treasurer of Stamford Historical Society Charged With Embezzlement," *Hartford Courant*, March 10, 2015, https://www.courant.com/breaking-news/hc-stamford-historical-society-embezzlement-arrest-0311-20150310-story.html.
12. "Former Yellowstone County Museum director admits taking $30,000," *Billings Gazette*, 2015, https://billingsgazette.com/news/state-and-regional/crime-and-courts/former-yellowstone-county-museum-director-admits-taking/article_0cc5c4e3-2ffb-5846-9859-1f3b269de2fb.html.
13. Megan Hiler, "SRI Exec. Director: embezzlement was 'heartbreaking'," WILX, May 1, 2019, https://www.wilx.com/content/news/SRI-Exec-Director—509339931.html.

14. Steve Johnson, "Former Field Museum employee admits to embezzling more than $400K," *Chicago Tribune*, January 4, 2016, https://www.chicagotribune.com/enter tainment/museums/ct-field-museum-embezzling-pleads-guilty-story.html.

15. Christopher Brewer, "Former Lewis County museum director suspect in $100,000 theft," *Seattle Times*, December 30, 2011, https://www.seattletimes.com/seattle -news/former-lewis-county-museum-director-suspect-in-100000-theft/.

16. *Nonprofit Fiscal Policies & Procedures: A Template and Guide* (CompassPoint Nonprofit Services, 2012), https://www.compasspoint.org/sites/default/files/documents /Guide%20to%20Fiscal%20Policies%20and%20%20Procedures.pdf.

17. Brian Alexander, "Controversy and Collections," *History News* 53 No. 2 (1998): 22.

18. Brian Alexander, "Draft notes on Collections Care Endowment at the Shelburne Museum," from the author's files, 1996.

19. "Policy," *Merriam-Webster*, accessed July 28, 2020, https://www.merriam-webster .com/dictionary/policy.

20. "Reporting and Operations," *Nonprofit Accounting Basics*, accessed July 28, 2020, https://www.nonprofitaccountingbasics.org/reporting-operations/policies.

21. "Creating Nonprofit Policies," *Board Source*, accessed July 28, 2020, https://board source.org/resources/creating-policies/.

22. Stephen Fishman, "What Governance Policies Should Your Nonprofit Have?" *NOLO*, https://www.nolo.com/legal-encyclopedia/what-governance-policies -should-your-nonprofit-have.html.

23. "Nonprofits and Sarbanes-Oxley," *ABA*, accessed July 28, 2020, https://www .americanbar.org/groups/center-pro-bono/resources/program-management /nonprofits_sarbanes_oxley/.

24. Rick Cohen, "Sarbanes-Oxley: Ten Years Later," *NonProfit Quarterly*, December 30, 2012, https://nonprofitquarterly.org/sarbanes-oxley-ten-years-later/#:~:text =What%20the%20Law%20Requires%20Only%20two%20provisions%20of ,seep%20from%20public%20corporations%20into%20the%20nonprofit%20sec tor%20.

25. "Timeline of events leading to Robert Archibald's Resignation," *STL Today*, December 21, 2012, https://www.stltoday.com/news/local/metro/timeline-of-events -leading-to-robert-archibald-s-resignation/article_8ed33112-8944-5c8d-8462 -75faa4b188a8.html.

26. "Board Roles and Responsibilities," National Council of Nonprofits, accessed July 28, 2020, https://www.councilofnonprofits.org/tools-resources/board-roles-and-re sponsibilities.

27. "Whistleblower Protections for Nonprofits," National Council of Nonprofits, accessed July 28, 2020, https://www.councilofnonprofits.org/tools-resources /whistleblower-protections-nonprofits.

28. *Tax-Exempt Organizations Alert: Whistleblower Policies*, DCBar Pro Bono Center, July 2017, https://www.lawhelp.org/files/7C92C43F-9283-A7E0-5931-E57134 E903FB/attachments/B2D746C6-B926-A6C3-DC91-9D2D7233A7AA /whistleblower-policy-alert-2017-update-final.pdf.

29. "Code of Ethics Law and Legal Definition," Code of Ethics, US Legal, accessed July 28, 2020, https://definitions.uslegal.com/c/code-of-ethics/.

30. Colin Moynihan, "Sanctions Are Imposed on Berkshire Museum for Sale of Artworks," *New York Times*, May 27, 2018, https://www.nytimes.com/2018/05/27/arts /design/berkshire-museum-sanctions-aamd.html.

31. AAMD, "AAMD Statement on Sanction of Berkshire Museum and La Salle University Art Museum," Association of Art Museum Directors, May 25, 2018, https://aamd.org/for-the-media/press-release/aamd-statement-on-sanction-of-berkshire-museum-and-la-salle-university.

32. AAM, "AAM Code of Ethics for Museums," accessed July 28, 2020, https://www.aam-us.org/programs/ethics-standards-and-professional-practices/code-of-ethics-for-museums/.

33. "Nonprofits and Sarbanes-Oxley," *ABA*, accessed July 28, 2020, https://www.americanbar.org/groups/center-pro-bono/resources/program-management/nonprofits_sarbanes_oxley/.

34. David Hunn, "Alderman seeks hearings on History Museum, Archibald," *STLToday*, December 14, 2012, https://www.stltoday.com/news/local/govt-and-politics/david-hunn/alderman-seeks-hearings-on-history-museum-archibald/article_e5bffe69-9c22-5261-b797-b51af27706f1.html.

35. "How Much Does It Cost to Defend an Employment Lawsuit?" *Workforce*, May 14, 2013, https://www.workforce.com/news/how-much-does-it-cost-to-defend-an-employment-lawsuit.

36. Debbie Dimery and Tamara Graham, "Essential Policies in a Nonprofit Organization," Lindquist CPA, April 5, 2018, https://www.lindquistcpa.com/insights/essential-policies-in-a-nonprofit-organization/#:~:text=%20Essential%20Policies%20in%20a%20Nonprofit%20Organization%20,may%20exist%20when%20a%20board%20member%2C...%20More%20.

37. Nick Price, "Nonprofit Board Confidentiality Policy," *Board Effect*, January 29, 2018, https://www.boardeffect.com/blog/nonprofit-board-confidentiality-policy/.

38. "Sample Confidentiality Agreements for Information about Clients," National Council of Nonprofits, accessed July 28, 2020, https://www.councilofnonprofits.org/sites/default/files/documents/SAMPLE%20Confidentiality%20Agreements.pdf.

39. "Sample Confidentiality Agreements for Information about Clients," National Council of Nonprofits, accessed July 28, 2020, https://www.councilofnonprofits.org/sites/default/files/documents/SAMPLE%20Confidentiality%20Agreements.pdf.

40. "Code of Ethical Standards," Code of Ethics, Association of Fundraising Professionals, accessed July 28, 2020, https://afpglobal.org/ethicsmain/code-ethical-standards.

41. "Form 990," IRS, accessed July 28, 2020, https://www.irs.gov/pub/irs-pdf/f990.pdf.

42. "Top Ten Policies and Practices for Nonprofit Organizations," Alerts and Resources, Montgomery McCracken Attorneys at Law, December 17, 2013, https://www.mmwr.com/alert-resource/top-ten-policies-and-practices-for-nonprofit-organizations/.

43. "Investment Policies for Nonprofits," National Council of Nonprofits, accessed July 28, 2020, https://www.councilofnonprofits.org/tools-resources/investment-policies-nonprofits#:~:text=Elements%20of%20a%20clearly%20defined%20investment%20policy%20statement,investment%20management%20advisory%20services%20and%20evaluate%20investment%20advisors%20.

44. "Investment Management for Non-Profit Organizations," Bradley, Foster & Sargent, Inc., accessed on July 28, 2020, http://www.bfsinvest.com/resources/our-clients/Revised_WhitePaper_Non-Profits_Investment%20Management%20Best%20Practices%2010-23-12.pdf.

45. Amy Coates Madsen, "The importance of having gift acceptance policies," *Maryland Nonprofits*, March 5, 2020, https://www.marylandnonprofits.org/the-importance-of-having-gift-acceptance-policies/.

46. Patricia A. O'Malley, "Internal Controls," *Reporting and Operations, Nonprofit Accounting Basics*, May 24, 2017, https://www.nonprofitaccountingbasics.org/reporting-operations/internal-controls.
47. "Internal Controls for Medium-Sized Organizations," *Reporting and Operations, Nonprofit Accounting Basics*, accessed July 28, 2020, https://www.nonprofitaccountingbasics.org/reporting-operations/internal-controls-medium-sized-organizations.
48. John L. Calcagni, "The Top 7 Embezzlement Cases in U.S. History," Law Office of John L. Calcagni, May 7, 2017, https://mass.calcagnilaw.com/top-5-embezzlement-cases-u-s-history/.
49. *Report to the Nations: 2020 Global Study on Occupational Fraud and Abuse*, Association of Certified Fraud Examiners, accessed July 28, 2020, https://www.acfe.com/report-to-the-nations/2020/.

7

Making Finance Everyone's Job

Most museums in the United States have fewer than five staff, and more than three-quarters have fewer than ten.[1] The principal reason for this is not lack of work, but lack of funding. Work is plentiful, but museum budgets are often disagreeably small and there is almost always a need for more employees. Because of limited staffing, museum workers assume a wide range of responsibilities. The typical small museum director, for example, is often a blend of administrator, curator, public relations specialist, researcher, exhibition curator, accountant, fundraiser, maintenance worker, and much more.

This problem is particularly acute because the majority of museums in the United States are independent nonprofits and do not have the infrastructure of a larger system to help support their activities. This often means there are inconsistent or nonexistent protocols for financial management, limited checks and balances, and sporadic financial oversight. Small organizations manage the best they can with the resources available.[2] An already-stretched staff may be assigned responsibilities with little time, training, or experience. As a result, many operational details are overlooked, neglected, deferred, or simply left undone because of overwhelming workloads. In those cases when there is no staff, trustees are left with both governance and operational responsibilities.

Slow, intermittent progress is possible in some areas of a museum's operation—examples might include upgrading collections storage, improving collections cataloging, or modernizing exhibitions to name a few—and, while slow progress is not desirable, it is not likely to create an existential crisis if attention is not constant. Finance, however, is different because it requires full and constant vigilance, especially when financial resources are scarce. The margin for error is slim, and the implications are enormous.

Diverting focus on finances for even a brief time makes the museum vulnerable and opens the door to increasingly serious problems. Momentary lapses of oversight or inattention to cash flow, financial reports, or record keeping may open the door to increasingly serious problems. Even when miscues are seemingly minor, they tend to be insidious and grow larger and more serious if not addressed. Diligence in all financial matters is central to an institution's well-being. Fortunately, much of finance is about attention and commitment. Financial management must be a priority, even for those institutions with limited resources.

Information sharing throughout an organization is an inexpensive and productive means of ensuring financial understanding and oversight. Access to budget and performance reports gives staff (or volunteers) a better understanding of institutional financial challenges and important perspectives on why decisions are made. It provides everyone with knowledge of financial matters and creates an environment in which there is financial ownership at every level of the organization. This is an important step that not only provides a broad and transparent level of financial oversight, but also builds staff morale and institutional solidarity.

Senior staff and trustees must lead the charge and be fully conversant with finances and the implications of their decisions, but a more shared approach results in more thorough consideration and better decisions. It also lessons the chances of fraud, theft, embezzlement, and other untoward activity because everyone is paying attention. Institutions must take the attitude that finances impact everyone and everyone has a responsibility to make the balance sheet a healthy one.

When financial resources are scarce, great skill is required to effectively manage an organization's finances. If lack of funding is a major issue that flirts with closing a museum's doors, when blended with a lack of know-how, few checks and balances, and limited planning, it likely will slam the door shut entirely. While not a mission-driven function, finances provide the means to make pursuit of the mission and continued viability possible. It is central to virtually every aspect of museum life.

INATTENTION OR INABILITY?

Ironically, management of financial resources is often not given the level of attention that it deserves. This may be a result of a lack of staff resources or training to properly focus on financial matters, disinterest or casual attitude toward financial matters, or a general lack of understanding by staff and trustees about the complexity or implications of an organization's financial decisions. It may also be caused by an attitude that finances are "not central to what the museum does" or are "someone else's responsibility." Not only does this attitude result in poor decisions and ineffective use of resources, but it sometimes leads to deliberate attempts to defraud the institution when it becomes clear that such wrongdoing might be easy to effect with little fear of being caught or prosecuted.

Trustees have the final say on a museum's financial matters. As fiduciaries, they assume ultimate oversight and responsibility for finances on behalf of the public they represent. They are responsible for approving and monitoring financial policies and investments; authorizing major funding initiatives; approving the annual operating budget; reviewing financial reports on a regular basis; providing general financial oversight; and ensuring long-term sustainability. They also ensure accountability to donors and the general public, as well as compliance with federal and state regulations.[3]

Despite the gravity and impact of financial management, not all decision-makers are equally engaged in financial matters, often ratifying budgets and other financial matters with relatively little scrutiny, discussion, or understanding. Reliance is often placed on the shoulders of the CEO and treasurer—important voices, but not the only ones. Broader perspective is critically important and an essential component of the shared governance model in nonprofit organizations. Yet in many cases there is not full engagement and understanding until circumstances *demand* participation because of a crisis that threatens the very existence of the museum. Then decisions are made with fewer alternatives and increasingly serious implications—and sometimes it is too late.

Trustees set the tone for how the museum perceives and manages its finances. Most do it responsibly and effectively, but it is important to consider the nature of trusteeship. Trustees are volunteers, engage on a level that works for them, and often find it infinitely more interesting and rewarding to discuss matters such as exhibitions and programs. Much of the responsibility for finance is left to the CEO and treasurer, but when the museum faces allegations of financial wrongdoing or other crises, the board is surprised that the museum finds itself in this position. Unfortunately, in many instances, the financial well-being of an organization is assumed to be good unless a catastrophic event suggests otherwise.

As a practical matter, much operational responsibility for finance is delegated to the CEO and staff. How well these financial responsibilities are handled by the staff is largely dependent on 1) the emphasis placed on prudent financial management dictated, modeled, and monitored by the trustees, and 2) staff resources, knowledge, capability, and trustworthiness necessary to properly execute those responsibilities.

Financial management is largely a "behind the scenes" activity and does not directly enhance the outward image of the museum. As a result, it does not always receive adequate attention or resources during times when institutions worry about public perception, competition for visitors, exhibition upgrades, program expansion, and other important priorities. It competes with other operational needs for funding and is often understaffed or duties are incorporated into other jobs as a result of institutional priorities or budget necessity.

Even when an effective financial management structure is in place, it does not guarantee success. Things do not always work out. Projecting revenues is not an exact science. Emergency, unplanned expenditures are often necessary. An economic downturn is beyond the museum's control. Embezzlement happens even among the most trusted staff. Ultimately, administrators must diligently focus on those things within their control and be prepared for those things that are not.

OVERSIGHT AND MANAGEMENT

OVERSIGHT

There are layers of trust involved in museum finance, and that trust begins with the general public who must trust the board (as fiduciary) to effectively manage the resources and finances of the museum on the public's behalf. Donors, foundations, and granting agencies must trust museum trustees to manage their contributions wisely and use funds to support the purposes for which they were given. The board of trustees, in turn, must trust the CEO (and by extension, the staff) to recommend sound policies and initiatives and manage approved budgets and other financial matters responsibly.

Trustee responsibility for finances is usually manifested through major decision-making; policy development and ratification; approval of operating budgets and major funding initiatives; investment matters; and general financial oversight. They make big decisions with far-reaching implications such as embarking on a major capital campaign or new building expansion. Such decisions, and the level of risk tolerance and confidence placed in them, should come from the representative body of the public (aka trustees) who have the responsibility for the ultimate short- and long-term welfare of the organization. Naturally they must consult with and rely on the professional expertise and knowledge of the CEO and staff (and outside consultants when appropriate).

Problems often originate at the oversight level, when trustees approve budgets that are not attainable or endorse revenue projections that are too aggressive. Sometimes there is eagerness to engage in a capital campaign without fully understanding the financial implications. Other times, too much reliance is placed on the judgment of only a few trustees or CEO, and other trustees do not express their concerns or hesitation. There are also times when decisions are made that are advantageous in the short-term—

using endowment principal to fund deficits as one example—without full consideration of the long-term implications. And at other times, there is little choice but to borrow money that will have far-reaching effects on subsequent budgets. Such decisions may or may not be the right course of action, but they should be given full and thorough discussion and not be left to a few individuals.

The concept of trust extends beyond the boardroom and CEO, with a great deal of operational financial management delegated to the staff at large. The CEO, as leader of the staff, trusts the staff to spend wisely and in accordance with approved budgets. The staff must trust the CFO (or equivalent) to accurately track, document, and report expenditures and revenues in the service of the approved direction mandated by the CEO through prescribed policies of the board. Each level of the operation must trust the other—the staff must trust the trustees to make sound policies, the trustees must trust the CEO's recommendations and ability to manage the budget, and all must trust that financial controls are adequate and provide valid information.

Regardless of budget size or trustee/staff expertise, financial control always relies to a great extent on trust, and like so many other areas of the museum—collections management and security as examples—a breach of trust can bring an organization to its knees.

Trust alone, however, is not enough to manage finances. There must be systems that provide effective oversight, checks and balances and policies and procedures to provide reasonable assurance that finances are being handled in a responsible fashion at every level. Every staff member must abide by these rules to ensure a thorough and systematic method of controlling finances. Everyone is affected by finance, and finance impacts the very viability of the museum. Finances are everyone's responsibility.

Daily operations see many transactions, and there may be insufficient or untrained staff to handle proper processing and financial monitoring. This leads to trouble, and finances become vulnerable. Employees know that limited oversight makes theft relatively easy to perpetrate. Directors and staff pressed for time sometimes take shortcuts from prescribed systems and procedures. Checks and balances slow things down. The limits and definition of appropriate expenditures gradually become blurred. The museum credit card is used for personal expenses and never reimbursed, either by design or neglect. The list goes on, and problems grow larger. The bottom line is that if everyone is not paying attention and fully engaged in their respective roles, a combustible situation is created that puts the long-term viability of the museum into serious jeopardy.

Research shows that deliberate fraud generally happens on the operational and staff level, where there are many small transactions with limited oversight. Those in charge of finance often work alone, which allows for an easy opportunity for embezzlement or other crimes. Generally, unquestioned trust is placed in those who handle financial matters, and there is often little oversight (or policies are in place but not followed). This category runs the full gamut from misusing company credit cards; forging checks; paying personal expenses from museum funds; stealing cash from donation boxes; staff giving themselves pay raises or making mysterious withdrawals from museum accounts; doctoring accounting ledgers; selling museum collections for personal financial gain; and scheming to mislead auditors. There are even instances of staff executing telemarketing schemes and submitting fraudulent health insurance claims.

Sometimes wrongdoing becomes tempting because monitoring finances may be left to the individual to monitor himself. It becomes entirely dependent upon the individual to make a judgment about whether a legal line is crossed because there is little likelihood of getting caught. The temptation may be too great. For example, it is relatively easy to steal cash when counting the day's receipts or emptying the donation box if the same individual does the record keeping. Instead of recording and depositing cash transactions, they are stolen. And it may become tempting for someone with check-writing authority to write museum checks to himself when there is no oversight. This is compounded when an employee has personal financial difficulties and harbors resentment over what he or she perceives as a relatively low or unfair salary.

When wrongdoing occurs, museum officials are typically shocked that a longtime, seemingly trustworthy employee would steal. Officials then immediately institute new, more stringent financial controls that should have been in place before wrongdoing occurred. In a sense, museum officials enable such behavior because through their lack of attention, they imply that finances are not important enough to provide careful monitoring and therefore stealing is probably not important either. It becomes an open invitation to steal.

Financial controls and oversight protect the employee *and* the institution. The institution is protected because it is more difficult for employees to contemplate stealing because transgressions are noticed quickly, and individuals are easily identified. For example, requiring two signatures on checks or two people counting cash are examples of control measures. One person acts as a check against the other. And the individual is protected because if cash can be accessed and counted only when two people are present, it is less likely that one person can be accused of stealing. Naturally collusion is always possible, but far less likely.

Financial wrongdoing is about more than losing money or staff violating the trust placed in them. The implications are much broader. It calls into question the competency and trustworthiness of the entire organization. It casts a shadow throughout the museum—if staff are stealing money, are they also stealing collections? Are annual gifts being stolen or used for improper purposes? Are donations being used to enrich the staff? Are the trustees and CEO competent? Can the museum be trusted? It is a blemish that does not go away easily. Constituencies must have confidence that the museum is handling its resources responsibly and is living up to its public trust obligations.

In 2019, police were looking for the former finance director of a museum in the Midwest whom authorities believed had embezzled over $200,000 from the museum. Officials believed the money was used for such personal purchases as gas, groceries, and other items dating back to 2016. The embezzlement was perpetrated when the finance director was given extra duties because the museum's executive director became ill and many of her responsibilities were distributed to coworkers.

When the executive director returned to work, museum officials noticed that some of the financials did not add up. They conducted an audit, and the results pointed to wrongdoing on the part of the finance director. "I trusted my finance director with some extra responsibility and basically . . . that situation that was taken advantage of," said the executive director. The finance director had worked at the museum for about seven years and had earned the trust of the organization. Museum officials found the embezzlement hard to believe. "It was very overwhelming. It was heartbreaking," according to the executive director. "We're not going to let anybody mess up what we've worked so very hard for," she said.[4] The finance director was eventually apprehended and sentenced.

The bookkeeper at a California museum was charged with embezzlement and grand theft of at least $25,000 during the period of 2013–2017 after a lengthy investigation. The theft was discovered when a new museum president was named and initiated a close examination of the museum's finances and bookkeeping practices. Among other things, investigators found missing pages in bank statements; checks amounting to thousands of dollars made payable to and deposited by the bookkeeper into her personal account; unapproved charges to the museum credit card for online purchases; membership fees that were recorded but not deposited in the accounting system; and numerous deposits entered into the financial records without actual corresponding deposits into the museum's bank account.

Even though the organization had a policy of checks and balances in which the bookkeeper was required to have checks reviewed and signed by two board members, museum officials did not always abide by that policy, and sometimes board members signed blank checks for the bookkeeper to pay bills or payroll. As a consequence, the bookkeeper wrote fraudulent checks to herself and used the museum credit card for personal purposes without authorization. The bookkeeper, in an attempt at contrition, attempted to pay restitution to the museum and apologized for betraying the trust of the museum and hoped the museum would "accept this financial restitution as a pitiful attempt to restore some element of repayment for my wrongdoing." The check, however, was kept as evidence by the authorities.[5]

Another example of a lapse in oversight was when a business manager at a children's museum in New England was charged with alleged embezzlement of $18,500 between 2016 and 2018. Museum officials, suspecting irregularities in its cash accounts, questioned the museum's business manager about financial management issues and missing money. As a result, she soon resigned. The museum then brought in individuals with financial backgrounds to more carefully review the organization's financial records, and they noticed "multiple irregularities," and believed that money had actually been *stolen* from the museum, according to the court papers. The financial review further indicated that during the two-year period, $58,322 in receipts were recorded as being taken in at the museum's cash register, but only $38,741 was actually deposited in the organization's bank account. The business manager was suspected because she was solely responsible for making all bank deposits. Police began an investigation after a complaint was filed by the museum and resulted in police obtaining a court warrant for the business manager's arrest.[6]

In addition to these common embezzlement activities, some employees were more creative in their activities. For example, the former director of a visual arts center pleaded guilty to stealing more than $130,000 from not just one, but two nonprofit organizations. She embezzled $98,000 from the local arts center and another $41,000 from the state museum association, where she served as treasurer. She was sentenced to two fifteen-year prison sentences, with six months behind bars and probation for the remainder of the sentence. In addition, she was required to pay $140,000 in restitution.[7] And in 2017, at an Australian museum the chief scientist and chief executive officer of the museum faced charges over a private health insurance scam in which she made over $45,000 in fraudulent health insurance claims over a three-year period.[8]

Sometimes staff members circumvent established procedures, exceed their authority, and pursue financial matters without required approvals because of a lack of oversight. Even when there is no direct personal financial benefit in doing this, there may be other motivations.

The former director of a Southwestern museum was found guilty on five counts of embezzlement and two counts of grand theft when it was discovered that he had removed 127 items worth approximately $2.2

million and illegally put them up for sale or trade. He asserted that he did so to use the proceeds to build the museum's collections with more important works. He claimed he received no personal benefit from these transactions, although such claims were disputed by the district attorney. The director portrayed himself at war with a dysfunctional and ineffective board, and his secret actions, such as falsification of inventories, were done in the best interests of the museum.[9]

It is not just small museums that fall victim to financial wrongdoing. Larger institutions have more complex finances, many income streams, and countless transactions every day, and lack of attention often leads to problems. In 2009 the former manager of payroll and accounting at a major New York museum was charged with stealing more than $600,000 as a result of issuing bogus paychecks that were funneled into the accounting manager's personal accounts.[10]

The crime was committed by issuing 138 checks to employees named "ZYX" or other fictitious names. Once issued, they were direct-deposited in the accounting manager's joint bank account with his wife, who was a retired detective. Ironically, she had worked previously with the local district attorney's office on various matters. They were both charged with wire fraud and faced up to twenty years in prison. According to one news article, the couple had a "troubled financial history." The museum stated that it planned to "vigorously seek restitution of the stolen funds," and take "swift action to assure that such a theft will not happen again." Apparently there was little to suspect the employee of committing a crime.[11]

One museum association fell victim to a scheme that embezzled over $700,000 from the association during the period of 2006–2010. Two individuals were criminally indicted for embezzlement and faced criminal charges and a civil lawsuit—which also named an accounting firm which the association accused of negligence. The association contacted authorities after it discovered "alarming" financial discrepancies within the organization and suspected its longtime financial manager of withdrawing six-figure amounts each year from the association's accounts over the four-year period. She was also accused of using company credit cards to purchase a range of items, including tickets to concerts and merchandise from the TV channel QVC. In addition, the organization sued its CPA auditing firm for failing to act when there were obvious signs of financial wrongdoing. The suit conceded that while the firm did identify several issues pertaining to the organization's finances—most notably that the financial manager had sole authority over funds—the company still "breached its duty . . . by failing to obtain reasonable assurance that all . . . financial statements it provided to the Plaintiff were free of material misstatement."

The suit sought nearly $4.9 million, which included repayment of the stolen funds, a $3-million compensatory award against the couple, and another $950,000 from the auditing firm.[12]

In Massachusetts, a chief financial officer pleaded guilty in 2010 to taking cash and creating credit accounts in the museum's name and making charges for personal use. She manipulated the museum's books to make it look as though the expenses were legitimate. Ultimately, she admitted to seventeen counts of larceny and credit card fraud, and one charge of making false corporate entries. The theft totaled $1.3 million over six years. Among other things, the stolen money funded college tuition for her children and clothes for herself. There was also a separate civil case brought by the museum for misappropriation of funds. The museum took notice and committed to tightening its financial controls. According to the head of the board of trustees, "This whole process clarified a number of things for us. I feel we have a far better understanding of our finances, and we're safer than we were before."[13]

Major criminal activity in museums is not the exclusive province of museums in the United States. In 2015 in Russia the ex-deputy culture minister, along with officials of several private companies involved in various cultural restoration projects, was charged with embezzlement through the willful corrupt management of various museum-related projects. During the execution of the contracts, over $900 million rubles (approximately $14 million dollars) were stolen as part of a conspiracy between the deputy culture minister and the contractors, who were charged with creating an organized criminal group to steal budget funds using their positions of authority.[14]

Often a casual attitude toward finances by museum leadership creates opportunities for financial misdeeds. Usually this begins when finances are relatively good and not a major concern. Reporting becomes routine, and financial matters are not fully discussed or carefully scrutinized. Complacency soon sets in, and decisions are made without full consideration of their implications. Quick decisions are made to approve major expenditures or aggressive revenue projections. Prescribed protocols are no longer strictly followed. Individuals begin to stretch the limits of their authority. There is a general level of inattention, and financial reports are only scanned at best.

All this leads to financial confusion and poor role modeling. Mixed messages about the importance of finance echo throughout the organization. Decisions seem arbitrary and inconsistent. There is a kind of benign neglect in financial management, even a sense of financial invincibility. Bolder and more unrestrained decision-making rule financial discussions. When museum leaders are not well-informed and willing to make decisions without careful scrutiny, bad things happen quickly and lay the groundwork for financial disasters of a large scale.

Trustees look to the CEO for his or her professional guidance and experience to help frame proposed initiatives and decision-making. But the CEO must be checked by the trustees, who bring a range of perspectives to the governance of the museum. They have a critical and legal responsibility to exercise financial oversight with "care." Relying too much on the CEO and senior staff also puts an unfair burden on them because they alone should not carry the burden of major decisions. Such decisions demand full participation and analysis by the trustees. Thorough discussion is essential to understand and analyze a range of perspectives to properly inform decisions. Everyone must exercise their proper shared roles for responsibility and accountability.

In 2011 in the State of Washington a former executive director was charged with ten counts of first-degree theft in connection with the disappearance of $460,000 in the museum's endowment fund over a three-year period. An investigation revealed that money had been transferred from the endowment fund to a personal bank account, with a debit card that was used to make "personal purchases of goods from local businesses, and services such as utility payments." Police also believed the executive director wrote checks to herself in excess of her salary. When the museum became aware of the funds' disappearance, all sitting executive board members were voted out of office and immediately resigned, leaving new leadership to take over. The new board "feared the worst" after discovering the museum's financial records did not reflect those obtained from its bank. Police began investigating the endowment withdrawals after museum officials suspected wrongdoing and turned in the museum's financial records from the museum's bank. As a consequence of the lack of oversight, the new executive board was forced to lay off paid staff, citing financial difficulties. The board reported just over $2,000 left in its primary bank account, with over $13,000 in unpaid bills. The board later voted to accept a "gracious" loan offer from its bank to help pay off the museum's debts. "This is sad because (executive director) has been our friend and she did so much for the museum," the new board president said. The museum bylaws called for two board members to sign off on any withdrawal from the endowment fund, but board members failed to follow policy. Such failure resulted in a scandal, a public-relations blemish, questions of institutional credibility, and loss of funds. It undoubtedly had an impact on donors and their confidence in the institution as well.[15]

In another episode, federal authorities in 2007 charged a former museum president with mail fraud and tax evasion, claiming that the individual defrauded the museum of more than $1 million over a nine-year period. According to authorities, the person created phony invoices and charged personal items to the museum, including a European vacation. The individual also used $50,000 of museum funds to personally purchase various rare artifacts. According to the U.S. Attorney, "He spent with reckless abandon, went to extraordinary lengths to conceal his fraudulent activities, and abused the trust placed in him by the museum."[16]

These are a few examples of how unfortunate things happen when there is unquestioned trust placed in someone who has financial access and authority. When coupled with little or no oversight, the potential for abuse is great. Certainly, the board must trust the senior staff to do its job, but there must always be an appropriate level of oversight to regularly review and monitor financial matters.

News of an alleged financial scandal was made by a major California art museum in 2015 when a whistleblower complaint by the museum's chief financial officer was made against the museum president (who was also acting as the museum's chief executive officer). According to the complaint, the board president signed off on (and got the chief financial officer to cosign) a "disability severance payment" of $450,000 to a retired staff member. The president allegedly did not seek the approval of the full board of trustees for this major expenditure.[17] The retired staff member was married to the museum's director of registration, who was "well-known for doing favors" for the board president. Apparently, the payment was signed off on by the chief financial officer, who assumed the full board had approved the payment. The retiree had already collected a $56,580 annual pension from the city, which provided major funding to the museum each year. The complaint was filed when the CFO feared she was being pushed out by the president as retaliation for questioning the propriety of the payment. Two board members resigned over the "lack of financial controls,"[18] and both the city and the state attorney general investigated the complaint of financial misconduct.[19]

This incident alone was probably enough to raise eyebrows and question the financial transparency of this nonprofit organization, but there were other financial-related issues surrounding the museum that created at the very least some serious public relations issues.[20] For example, there were several firings of longtime senior staff apparently without warning or cause, which one employee described as "deceptive and unprofessional"; claims that a painting valued at approximately $500,000 was purposely valued at only $15,000 to save $35,000 in customs fees[21]; accusations that the president was using museum staff time and other resources to manage, photograph, and ship her personal art collection; and changing museum bylaws to eliminate term limits for the board president.[22]

In another case, a museum director was removed from her position over conflict-of-interest allegations. According to allegations, the director paid only a nominal sum for a designer wedding dress that she purchased as part of a quid pro quo arrangement for promoting the works of the dress designer. In addition, she was accused of receiving a free rental for her wedding at an elegant rental venue in in return for providing the rental venue organization with free use of space at the museum. While some believed that this was a clear quid pro quo and a violation of museum conflict-of-interest policies, both charges were denied. Her removal had significant repercussions and losses of funding from trustees and donors who disagreed with the decision. Six trustees immediately resigned in protest. One donor said that she felt so strongly about what she perceived as an injustice to the director that she planned to remove the museum from her will, which amounted to a "substantial amount of money."[23] Such activities that may be perceived as potential conflicts of interest require thorough vetting to avoid similar problems.

The same is true of accepting major gifts that have broad implications. Museums are always eager to accept a major gift from a wealthy donor, but sometimes that gift brings with it negative baggage that undermines the museum's very credibility. In times of financial stress, it is especially difficult for museums to turn away even potentially problematic gifts, but the perceptions that are created when the donor is revealed puts the museum in a position that challenges its credibility and honesty. Then follows a public relations debacle that affects the museum's reputation and continued support by constituents.

At the American Museum of Natural History (AMNH) in New York City, billionaire donor Rebekah Mercer left her position on the board in 2020, where she had served since 2013. Mercer, who gave millions to the museum, was a known climate change denier who faced increased pressure from the scientific community and two dozen of AMH's own curators to resign as a result of a perceived conflict between her views and the integrity of scientific research.[24] The scientific community believed that AMNH should "end ties to anti-science propagandists and funders of climate science misinformation, and to have Rebekah Mercer leave the American Museum of Natural History Board of Trustees." In an open letter addressed to the museum, scientists wrote: "When some of the biggest contributors to climate change and funders of misinformation on climate science sponsor exhibitions in museums of science and natural history, they undermine public confidence in the validity of the institutions responsible for transmitting scientific knowledge" . . . and accepting money from and giving power and legitimacy to a mega-funder of climate science denial, because it created signs of "skepticism" and "corruption."[25]

In a related case, billionaire David Koch left the AMNH after twenty-three years as a trustee and millions in gifts amid petitions and signatures of 52,000 names. Koch, too, was connected to the climate change denier movement, and scientists protested that "This corporate philanthropy comes at too high a cost." Koch was also involved in related controversies at the Smithsonian National Museum of Natural History and the Metropolitan Museum of Art.[26]

Whether or not there were ethical issues and financial improprieties in these stories is perhaps less important than the negative repercussions of *perceived* conflicts of interest. The very question of impropriety, lack of transparency, accusations of self-dealing, or conflicts with ethical standards can have a deleterious impact on an institution, its reputation, and continued support by donors and the public. Being as broadly transparent as possible is critical.

SUMMARY

While it is difficult to make generalizations, organizations that are most successful take finances seriously at every level of the organization, are transparent with the staff and public about financial difficulties, and have boards that are fully engaged in the financial management of the museum. They are self-monitoring and create informal and formal sets of checks and balances. They proceed in a forward-moving, but cautious and well-considered manner and encourage broad considerations of options. And perhaps above all, trustees and staff are willing to be realistic and honest with themselves.

Museum financial challenges are a constant. But if staff, the CEO, and trustees all assume a serious level of responsibility and accountability for the financial welfare of an organization (in good times and bad); have clear knowledge of an organization's capacity to grow and perform; not assume the "fatal mistake that funding will come—somehow, somewhere—because we deserve it;" and agree that finance is something that "we must talk about openly and honestly;" they will likely find themselves in a strong position.[27] Ultimately, as American Alliance of Museums (AAM) CEO Laura Lott noted in her remarks at the 2019 Annual Meeting of the AAM, "Financial sustainability is everyone's responsibility."[28]

ORGANIZATIONS THAT ENJOY SUCCESS:

Recognize that they are responsible to the public and the public should have a voice through the trustees and other means.

Ensure that everyone, at every level of the organization, has a reasonable understanding of museum financial needs and challenges.

Realize that trustees set the tone for financial management and through their actions model that attitude to the staff, public, and funders.

Know that finance is not an occasional job; ongoing attention is essential.

Take seriously conflicts of interest and ensure that they are managed appropriately.

Keep the integrity and credibility of the institution in the forefront at all times.

NOTES

1. "Small Museums," American Alliance of Museums, accessed May 26, 2020, http://ww2.aam-us.org/about-us/what-we-do/small-museums.
2. Ford W. Bell, *How Are Museums Supported Financially in the U.S.?* (United States Department of State Bureau of International Information Programs, 2012), https://photos.state.gov/libraries/amgov/133183/english/P_You_Asked_How_Are_Museums_Supported_Financially.pdf.
3. "Where can I find information on a board's legal duties?" Knowledge Base, Grantspace by Candid, accessed May 26, 2020, https://grantspace.org/resources/knowledge-base/legal-duties-of-the-nonprofit-board/.
4. Megan Hiler, "SRI Exec. Director: embezzlement was 'heartbreaking'," *WILX*, May 01, 2019, https://www.wilx.com/content/news/SRI-Exec-Director—509339931.html.
5. Gazette Staff, "Former bookkeeper at museum is charged with embezzlement," *Mariposa Gazette*, February 22, 2018, https://www.mariposagazette.com/articles/former-bookkeeper-at-museum-is-charged-with-embezzlement/.
6. Andrew Gorosko, "Woman Charged in EverWonder Embezzlement Case," *Newton Bee*, October 4, 2018, https://www.newtownbee.com/10042018/woman-charged-in-everwonder-embezzlement-case/.
7. Ty Watwood, "Former Arts Center Director Pleads Guilty to Theft," *WHNT*, May 7, 2012, https://whnt.com/news/decatur/former-arts-center-director-pleads-guilty-to-theft/.
8. Peter Devlin, "'Incredibly successful' chief scientist and museum boss, 52, charged with dishonestly claiming $45,000 worth of private health insurance," *Daily Mail*, July 24, 2017, https://www.dailymail.co.uk/news/article-4727074/Queensland-Museum-CEO-stood-fraud-charges.html.
9. David Colkler, "Ex-Director Convicted of Stealing Items From Museum: Embezzlement: He secretly sold or traded from the Southwest's collection worth hundreds of thousands of dollars," *Los Angeles Times*, March 11, 1993, https://www.latimes.com/archives/la-xpm-1993-03-11-me-1074-story.html.
10. U.S. Department of the Treasury, Internal Revenue Service, Form 990 (Washington, DC: 2017), https://pdf.guidestar.org/PDF_Images/2018/111/672/2018-111672743-10d5d5b9-9.pdf.
11. John Marzulli and Helen Kennedy, "Ex-payroll manager at Brooklyn Museum busted in $600G scam," *NY Daily News*, June 5, 2009, https://www.nydailynews.com/news/crime/ex-payroll-manager-brooklyn-museum-busted-600g-scam-article-1.376544.
12. "CPAs named in nonprofit embezzlement suit," *Nashville Post*, https://www.nashvillepost.com/home/article/20465571/cpas-named-in-nonprofit-embezzlement-suit.
13. Bruce S. Trachtenberg, "Nonprofit Newswire-Fraud in Fruitlands—Museum Comes Late to Financial Controls," *NonProfit Quaterly*, May 7, 2010, https://nonprofitquarterly.org/nonprofit-newswire-fraud-in-fruitlandsmuseum-comes-late-to-financial-controls/.
14. "New case against former culture top official to be heard in St. Petersburg," *RAPSI*, April 16, 2020, http://rapsinews.com/judicial_news/20200416/305721032.html.
15. Christopher Brewer, "Former Lewis County museum director suspect in $100,000 theft," *Seattle Times*, updated December 30, 2011, https://www.seattletimes.com/seattle-news/former-lewis-county-museum-director-suspect-in-100000-theft/.

16. John Shiffman, "Former Independence Seaport Museum director charged," *Philadelphia Inquirer*, May 21, 2007, https://www.inquirer.com/philly/news/breaking/20070521_Former_Independence_Seaport_Museum_director_charged.html.
17. Riley McDermid, "De Young Museum's CFO accuses Dede Wilsey of financial mismanagement, report says," *San Francisco Business Times*, October 19, 2015, https://www.bizjournals.com/sanfrancisco/morning_call/2015/10/fiscal-mismanagement-dede-wilsey-de-young-museum.html.
18. Matier and Ross, "De Young's Dede Wilsey under fire for payout to ex-museum worker," *SFGate*, October 19, 2015, https://blog.sfgate.com/matierandross/2015/10/19/de-youngs-dede-wilsey-under-fire-for-payout-to-ex-museum-worker/.
19. Riley McDermid, "De Young Museum's CFO accuses Dede Wilsey of financial mismanagement, report says," *San Francisco Business Times*, October 19, 2015, https://www.bizjournals.com/sanfrancisco/morning_call/2015/10/fiscal-mismanagement-dede-wilsey-de-young-museum.html.
20. Ruth Osborne, "The Business Of Museums: Mismanagement at the De Young in San Francisco," *Art Watch International*, https://www.artwatchinternational.org/the-business-of-museums-mismanagement-at-the-de-young-in-san-francisco/.
21. "Morale, management, and money," *San Francisco Bay Guardian*, February 26, 2013, http://sfbgarchive.48hills.org/sfbgarchive/2013/02/26/morale-management-and-money/.
22. "Mrs Wilsey's fine art," *San Francisco Bay Guardian*, February 26, 2013, http://sfbgarchive.48hills.org/sfbgarchive/2013/02/26/mrs-wilseys-fine-art/.
23. Robin Pogrebin, "6 Cooper Hewitt Trustees Resign After Director's Removal," *New York Times*, February 17, 2020, https://www.nytimes.com/2020/02/17/arts/design/cooper-hewitt-resignations.html.
24. Sarah Cascone, "Rebekah Mercer, Billionaire Donor to Anti-Science Causes, Is Off the American Museum of Natural History's Board After Years of Protest," *ArtNet News*, February 24, 2020, https://news.artnet.com/art-world/rebekah-mercer-off-american-museum-natural-history-board-1785090.
25. "Open Letter from Scientists to the American Museum of Natural History," *Natural History Museum*, January 25, 2018, http://thenaturalhistorymuseum.org/open-letter-from-scientists-to-the-american-museum-of-natural-history/.
26. Sarah Cascone, "Scientists Tell Natural History Museums to Shun Billionaire Donor and Climate Change-Denier David Koch," *ArtNet News*, March 25, 2015, https://news.artnet.com/exhibitions/david-koch-natural-history-museums-281214.
27. Laura Lott, "Financial Sustainability Is Everyone's Responsibility," *American Alliance of Museums*, May 29, 2019, https://www.aam-us.org/2019/05/29/financial-sustainability-is-everyones-responsibility/.
28. Laura Lott, "Financial Sustainability Is Everyone's Responsibility," *American Alliance of Museums*, May 29, 2019, https://www.aam-us.org/2019/05/29/financial-sustainability-is-everyones-responsibility/.

8

Moving Forward

Every museum has financial challenges. None ever has enough money. Whether it is searching for support to fund routine operations, cultivating donors to raise funds for a much-needed expansion, seeking grants to sponsor a special exhibition, or finding funds to make an emergency infrastructure repair, museums find themselves in a never-ending state of fundraising and income-generating activity. The size and extent of financial challenges vary, but nearly all museums find common ground in their need to create and develop revenue streams.

In looking at hundreds of news stories, there were recurring patterns of typical financial issues facing museums. It became apparent from examining these stories that there was a short list of surprisingly simple and obvious truths every organization can use to help minimize its financial challenges. While the list does not presume to be definitive in providing a road map to financial success, it does represent closely related ideas that may be helpful with relatively little effort or expense. Here are eight things to keep in mind:

BE AWARE OF THE RELATIONSHIP BETWEEN MONEY AND MISSION

The nature and focus of a museum's business is to enrich lives. Unlike for-profit businesses, creating income is not a museum's main priority. Instead, museums are driven by a mandate to serve the broad public interest and make their services widely accessible. This means making every effort to provide services that are affordable, yet still meaningful and relevant. It is a tricky balance.

Relying exclusively on funding generated directly from mission-related activities does not usually produce sufficient income to pay for the important services a museum provides because the costs of doing so make museum services prohibitively expensive to a museum's audience. This may result in a significant reduction in public access to a museum's programs and severely impairs a museum's ability to achieve its mission.

To make services possible, museums knowingly enter into what are often expensive mission-related activities with full knowledge that users will likely pay only a portion of the actual costs. Frequently it is the case that a program's best-case financial scenario is that its costs and revenues will break even, never mind generate a profit. As an example, the Association of Art Museum Directors noted in a 2015 survey that the total cost to an art museum of providing services to the average visitor was $55.25, but the income from each visitor amounted to only $11.72 (admissions, retail sales, and food service), or a net loss of $43.53 for each visitor![1]

As a result of revenue gaps such as these, museums must look beyond their direct users for help in making museum services sustainable or even possible. This support usually comes in various combinations of annual fund, planned giving, grant writing, major gifts, corporate and foundation support, endowment, sponsorships, memberships, as well as earned activities such as retail sales, food service, and facility rentals, to name just a few.[2]

It is reasonable to expect that direct users provide some support, but it must be supplemented by funding from others who view the museum as an important enhancement to the quality of life and economic well-being of the community. Outside funding must be sought from individuals and organizations who are willing to support the important work of the museum. Yet to attract this funding, museums must provide a quality product and make themselves important to the audiences they serve. It is a kind of catch-22 situation in which potential funders base their decisions to fund a museum on the level of quality services that the museum provides and its value to the community, yet museums cannot achieve this level of accomplishment unless funding is available to them.

Enhancing mission-driven activities without regard for financial constraints is not sustainable and quickly lands a museum in deep financial trouble. No organization has the resources to do this. Mission-related decisions, no matter how worthy, must be looked at in the context of financial resources, and decisions must be made with financial constraints in mind. The opposite is also true. Simply finding more ways to generate revenue is not the problem. That is too easy. Every organization is capable of being creative and devising lucrative revenue streams if the motivation is purely revenue generation and is unfettered by tax-exempt status, appropriateness, mission, and institutional credibility. Instead, such decisions must be made in the context of mission and preserving the dignity and integrity of the museum. There is a fine line between implementing mission while simultaneously generating funding streams that are appropriate and preserve institutional integrity and the confidence of the public.

Managing a nonprofit museum requires individuals who can deftly and simultaneously develop, manage, and measure both its important mission imperatives *and* its financial well-being. Finances largely dictate the nature and extent of mission-related activity, but finance is only important to the extent that it serves the museum mission. Finance and mission are always interdependent and must work together harmoniously if the museum is to be successful.

LOOK BEFORE YOU LEAP

Museums often struggle with finances because of a desire to expand and improve their services to the public. They are eager to offer innovative programming, present new exhibitions, make their facilities more visitor-friendly and safe, expand accessibility, preserve the collections, and create reasonable working conditions to attract a high-quality staff. The logical extension of this thinking is that these expansion activities and other enhancements will generate new revenue streams by drawing many new visitors.

Sometimes eagerness to provide new or expanded services creates unintended financial consequences that become untenable. In order to grow and expand, museums sometimes pursue projects they cannot afford and are forced to borrow heavily or draw from reserves or even endowment to cover expenses. And they realize too late that revenue projections for the operation of the new facility are too optimistic and thus are forced to reduce both the existing operation and the expansion. Funders become disillusioned because the new operation is not providing the level of service that was promised. The public is disappointed, and public relations suffer. The museum soon finds itself in a crisis situation, often in a worse financial state than before the expansion. The great irony is that museums expand to enhance services and generate more revenue, but the additional expense created by the expansion, coupled with unrealized operational revenue projections, often force dilution or even elimination of many services.

Premature or ill-considered expansion has gotten many institutions into financial trouble because they expanded before a solid financial foundation for expansion was in place. Sometimes anticipated revenue projections for future operation were too optimistic. It is important to remember that tomorrow always comes, and after the glitz and excitement of the expansion passes, there will be the day-to-day realities of operational costs. This means that when public expectations are at their highest, museum finances will be stretched to their limit. Sometimes the goal of making the museum better often has the opposite effect.

Undisciplined operational budgeting is another area that often comes back to haunt organizations. Since revenue budgets are the most speculative and unpredictable, and there is never a guarantee that revenue projections will be realized, conservative revenue budgeting is essential—

even if it means making painful decisions. It is important to know the limits of what an organization can risk if its revenue projections are not met. One can appreciate the desirability of preparing an optimistic operating budget to advance mission initiatives, but like expansion, tomorrow always comes, and one may have the very unpleasant task of making drastic corrections to balance the budget. And the longer one waits to make budget adjustments, the more difficult the challenge. Unrealistic revenue projections may result in the museum drawing from financial reserves or borrowing to cover the deficit—and the downward cycle begins.

Organizations cannot realistically plan for every exigency because many unanticipated things happen during the course of a year. Infrastructure failure, major repairs, and unexpected opportunities are likely to happen from time to time and can't always be predicted. This is why it is so important to plan for and manage those things that *can be* reasonably predicted. Pretending that some issues are not urgent and deferring them is dangerous because problems will only get worse, expenses will grow, a new set of problems will emerge, and financial problems will keep compounding. It is imperative to address and manage those things within our control and *do it realistically*. These events don't need to be exacerbated with unrealistic revenue projections or risky spending. Be honest and realistic with your budgets and know your organization's risk tolerance.

LEARN FROM OTHERS

There are hundreds of case studies and news reports of institutions that encountered financial difficulties over the last several decades, especially during the difficult days of COVID-19. Some are still struggling, and others unfortunately never recovered, but many rebounded from difficult circumstances. These organizations became more resourceful and found ways to rethink the use of their resources to develop innovative sources of revenue. They developed cost-effective approaches to maintain their relevance and add more diversified revenue streams. Each story, whether ultimately successful or not, offers a window into the range of financial issues faced by museums and how they were handled. Each provides a lesson about the kinds of things that can happen to any organization. Awareness is perhaps the greatest teacher to help guide us through our financial challenges.

Naturally, every museum is different and has its own challenges and circumstances, but every museum can benefit in some way from the obstacles and triumphs experienced by others. The size or discipline of the museum does not seem to matter. Issues range from the trivial to the existential, but there are elements in each that help create a clearer understanding of the financial world of museums. Each story provides a new addition to our understanding and future navigation of similar challenges.

It is striking from reading stories that many problems can be minimized with little more than dedicated attention and oversight. Many issues are self-imposed and can be avoided, but the first step is recognition of what the typical issues are, how they happen, and what organizations have done to fix them. Hopefully, familiarity with what others have experienced will help museums avoid similar difficulties.

It is important to remember that every organization is vulnerable to financial missteps and at some point may experience some of the challenges faced by others. Reading about the misfortunes encountered by other organizations should be a reminder of what can happen. Whether it is a story of overly optimistic revenue projections, lack of oversight, questionable ethics, unaffordable expansion, confusion about authority, criminal misconduct, or successful innovation and entrepreneurship, diversification of revenue sources, successful expansion, and full utilization of resources, there are plenty of lessons to be learned.

Put aside a few minutes each day to learn what others are doing well, what challenges they face, and how they addressed them. Even if stories do not specifically mimic your own circumstances, they provide important insights into how others have dealt with trying times.

BE REALISTIC AND DON'T DEFER DIFFICULT DECISIONS

"An ounce of prevention is worth a pound of cure" is a familiar axiom and one that is certainly applicable to museum finance. Human nature is such that we want to look at potential positive outcomes in most things we do, and we often create false realities that help convince us that we can achieve them. We convince ourselves that we can afford a new car, a bigger house, or a lavish vacation. This often involves a plan that makes every variable fit neatly into place and the future evolving just as we imagine. We focus on the upsides and dismiss or deemphasize the downsides. The problem is that things rarely play out according to plan. Life happens in our personal lives, and life happens in our professional lives. There is a rainy stretch of weather, a new construction project creates detours to the museum, a major employer closes and thousands of people (and museum visitors) lose their jobs, and the local government decides it can no long subsidize part of the museum's budget. Then we become burdened with committed expenditures with no way of paying for them. Future prospects of revenue are significantly diminished, budget cuts are necessary, and so begins a cycle of reduced services. What started as rosy optimism quickly becomes desperate pessimism.

Being realistic is the opposite of this. We begin by making choices that may be somewhat painful and unpopular because we are not deluded by vague prospects of increased revenues. Instead, we demand compelling evidence that we can achieve our revenue projections, and we monitor them closely against expenditures. We do not allow spending to get too far ahead of revenues, and we do not make major long-term commitments that we cannot afford. We are willing to take calculated risks, but not existential risks. Sometimes we must just say no. This is hard to do, of course, and often painful because there are so many things we want and need to do. Yet a dose of caution is worth it in the longer term because a financial crisis has likely been averted.

Deferring tough decisions is nourishment for catastrophe because avoiding them tends to make them grow. Then they become too big to handle, and drastic measures are necessary. Deferring difficult decisions does not make the problem go away; instead, it compounds the problems and makes them more difficult and harder to manage. There becomes less room to maneuver, options are more limited, and organizations are forced into a financial corner.

Don't be swayed by the prospect of doing new things if they put you at risk financially. Grow in a measured fashion and build upon small successes. Don't take a leap until you are fully confident it will work. Risk is fine, but risk only that which you can reasonably afford. Swinging for the fences may result in a strikeout. Budget conservatively and realistically and ask yourself if you would take such risks with your own personal finances. And remember, leaders must always have their eye on future horizons and sustainability, not just short-term gratification.

Every organization has its own set of needs and dreams for the future. They can be physical, programmatic, or operational expansion. They may be quite legitimate and make perfect sense. Just remember that the repercussions of getting ahead of yourself financially may be far-reaching and bring with them unintended results that could be existential in nature. Be willing to say no or demand solid justifications that a new direction will work. Don't put yourself at more risk than you can absorb if things don't go according to plan. Don't be afraid to make difficult decisions or slow down unbridled and unproven enthusiasm.

EMBRACE ENTREPRENEURSHIP EARLY

There is nothing quite like a crisis to unleash creativity and force action. When backs are against the wall and an urgent response is required, there is no better motivation to take decisive action to alleviate a problem. We hurriedly call upon our intellectual and experiential reserves to think of alternative ways to address problems. We do this under great duress because the urgency of the situation demands it. We feel free to abandon traditions and other limitations to become more "entrepreneurial." The pandemic is an example of this kind of urgent entrepreneurship. Museums had no choice but to respond quickly; some were able to do it well, and others did not have the wherewithal to develop an effective response. Waiting until disaster hit made measured, thoughtful experimentation more difficult and left many with few choices.

Entrepreneurship is about trial and error, testing, rethinking, revising, and refining. It takes time to do it well. We need time to fail and learn from our failures; failure is an essential element of entrepreneurship. While a crisis may force action, it often means *immediate* action and solutions. This makes it a high-risk proposition because successful entrepreneurship means reducing and not increasing risk. There is always some risk in entrepreneurship, of course, but it must be thoroughly considered and well-calculated. And this takes time and effort.

Without experimentation and testing, we are forced to provide services before they are ready, and the risk of failure is greatly increased. While it forces us to get to market quickly, we are well-advised not to do it too quickly. While a certain sense of urgency is a good thing and keeps us on our toes, we need to put ourselves in an ongoing cycle of entrepreneurship. It should be part of everyday life in museums and be part of institutional culture. Anticipating change and our response to it is critical. Waiting for a crisis before acting encourages recklessness, and boundaries are pushed too far and too fast. We risk more than is prudent.

It is easy to see why most museums are not naturally risk-takers and often take little risk unless forced to do so. Resources of staff and money are precious, and there are institutional traditions and expectations of audiences. Entrepreneurship may imply that the current institutional direction or mission is not being effectively achieved because "we have always done it this way." Thus there is relatively little risk-taking when times are good because there is not a compelling reason to do so; however, this is exactly when we should take some risks because we are not in a crisis situation. We have the benefit of time and money to properly experiment and move in new directions without "desperation entrepreneurship" forcing our hand. We are in a better position to grow organically, experiment thoughtfully, learn from our mistakes, and continue to improve our ideas or move in new directions.

Some risks, of course, are just too big, even in good times. Reckless projections, too-aggressive expansion and careless spending are prescriptions for disaster. Good times don't last forever; there will always be lean times and financial challenges. Most museums are not in a position to take big risks because there may not be a fallback position—"only gamble what you can afford to lose," but better yet, reduce your risks as much as possible so there is relatively little gambling involved. Successful entrepreneurship doesn't embrace high risk; it minimizes it.

Embrace entrepreneurship when healthy. Be ahead of the curve. Experiment. Anticipate the future. Think about collaborations and partnerships. Think about new directions but know the limits of your risk-taking. Know your competitive advantages and think about how to effectively exploit them in the marketplace. Be aggressive and entrepreneurial, but don't put your organization in an irreversible position.

EVALUATE DIVERSIFICATION CAREFULLY

Every organization strives for long-term and predictable sources of income, but sometimes too much reliance is placed on one or two sources that traditionally have been the foundation of an organization's financial sustainability. When those key sources are threatened, an organization's financial stability is rocked because there is no obvious way to replace what has been the very bedrock of an institution's revenue mix.

These changes may happen gradually, but often they happen quickly and without warning. The state of the economy suddenly changes, governmental funding for cultural organizations is reduced, funding priorities of donors are refocused on new funding interests, or they simply no longer have the financial wherewithal to maintain funding at current levels. Many other complications exist that throw revenue streams into turmoil, including an institution's ability to continually attract new and existing audiences, sustained periods of inclement weather (especially for outdoor museums), or major infrastructure repairs that force changes in budget priorities. The list goes on, and finding sources to support major gaps in revenue is not easy.

It is made more difficult because focusing on the likelihood of losing what has been a long-standing, major source often does not seem like a priority. It has always been there, and we hope it will continue to be there. Besides, most museums are too busy trying to sustain, manage, and stabilize those sources that traditionally have been more volatile rather than being too focused on what has been a reliable revenue source.

The obvious answer to all of this, of course, is not to put all of a museum's revenue eggs in one basket and instead diversify sources of revenue so the museum is not overly reliant on just one or two. Yet revenue diversification is a complex proposition that carries with it many competing and interrelated ramifications.

Some institutions do not vigorously pursue all potential revenue streams because they do not have the financial resources to properly fund them. Establishing a retail sales operation, for example, seems like a sound idea on the surface, but it takes considerable investments of inventory, space, merchandising, staffing, sales management, and more to make it possible. Food service is another example. It requires strategic purchasing of food and menu management, preparation and refrigeration equipment, staffing, and knowledge of sanitary and health issues required by law. Both of these activities require significant resources to become sustainable, and the initial investment can be enormous and beyond the means of many organizations. And if these initiatives are done on a more modest level, only modest returns can be expected. This calls into question whether such initiatives make sense. The same can be said of fundraising initiatives. These require staff, customer-relations management software, prospect research, planning, cultivation, execution, and more. And it takes time and money with no guarantee of success. It is not surprising that organizations rely on what has been successful in the past and hope they will continue to be successful in the future.

Revenue streams do not live in isolation from each other. Even if successful, organizations must consider the impact a new revenue stream may have on existing streams. Will donors feel their contributions are no longer necessary if they see a new museum store operation or café? Will these new operations take precious resources away from managing existing revenue streams? What is the return on investment? Is it short- or long-term? Does it take staff time away from other important initiatives?

Every revenue stream has varying degrees of predictability. Some sources are highly volatile while others remain relatively stable from year to year. Some areas may have potential to earn high revenues, but they may also be subject to high risk. Others may be less risky, but also may show relatively little growth. Unearned income is dependent on the economy and donors' inclination to give. This can fluctuate wildly from year to year. Earned income is dependent on a competitive marketplace and the appeal of museum programs and services and even the weather, to name just a few considerations. There are plenty of risks to go around—and they are often beyond the control of the museum.

When one considers that a museum's survival is often predicated on achieving a careful balance of revenue, it is easy to see that institutions balance themselves on a very thin line between success and failure, and when one source is no longer forthcoming, it may lead to a funding crisis.

One thing is certain. Revenue diversification can be a good thing, but it must be managed carefully with thoughtful examination of return on investment and impact on other activities. Proceed carefully.

PAY ATTENTION AND TAKE RESPONSIBILITY

It is ironic that financial management often is not given the level of attention that it deserves. This may happen for a number of reasons, such as lack of financial understanding or a casual attitude or lack of interest in financial matters. It could also be because of a lack of staff or resources to properly handle these "behind the scenes" duties. Or perhaps it is because finance is viewed as an obstacle that prevents the real business of the museum from happening. The reasons do not matter because they are just excuses.

Any museum, large or small, can effectively manage and protect the precious resources under its control. It can be more deliberate in its financial discussions and decision-making and more conservative and realistic with revenue projections. It can also take steps to carefully manage limitations on spending, establish measures to minimize the possibility of fraud, make financial decisions with reason rather than emotion, and plan carefully for its future. Much of this work requires that we make finance a priority and ensure that it receives careful consideration and consistent oversight. It is a relatively inexpensive investment that pays huge dividends.

Deciding that financial management is a priority and central to the well-being of the museum flows first from the trustees and affects all layers of the organization. Trustees are the role models for how the museum views finance. They must demonstrate that their organization stays true to its mission-related purposes, its resources are being used wisely, and business is conducted honestly, transparently, and ethically. It is not just a matter of keeping accurate records, but about taking responsibility for financial decisions and fully understanding the importance they occupy in the life of the museum. Trustees set the tone for the level of financial vigilance and how the museum manages financial matters.

Lack of consistent attention to finance is insidious. Small problems have a way of growing into big problems, and big problems become increasingly difficult to manage because the stakes become so much higher. Waiting too long to identify problems and take corrective action can be a waste of resources because it forces drastic action that could have been dealt with simply had it been addressed earlier.

Despite the gravity and impact of financial monitoring and decision-making, not all decision-makers are equally engaged in financial matters, often ratifying budgets and financial matters with relatively little scrutiny, discussion, or full understanding of their implications. Asking questions, reading monthly reports, understanding inconsistencies, insisting on credible projections, and managing budget progress carefully are key. Reading and understanding IRS Form 990 and the annual audit are important as well. This leads to informed decision-making and helps ensure that strong financial management is a pillar of museum success and sustainability.

Careful financial review and questioning should not be looked at as an impediment to moving things forward, but rather as an important tool to get things done. It helps us make responsible decisions that, while not foolproof, greatly reduce the likelihood of catastrophic failure or even institutional collapse. Decisions that may seem harsh in the beginning will likely result in decisions that are less harsh and cataclysmic in the end. Also, without careful attention it becomes too easy to assign blame or responsibility for financial failures because no real ownership is ever taken because of a seeming lack of concern.

Allowing financial focus to wane, whether deliberately or otherwise, can lead the museum down the wrong road, and sometimes there is no way back. Lack of oversight, careless spending, poor record keeping, casual review of reports, unrealistic revenue projections, or incomplete consideration of the implications of a major expansion are among the things that can quickly put an organization on the fast track to catastrophe. There must be constant and careful oversight, standardized internal controls, and thoughtful decision-making and information sharing on every level.

Museums can and must do more than just hope that things turn out well. They must put systems and oversight mechanisms in place not to prevent progress, but to make certain that progress is managed in a measured and responsible way. Museums must take seriously how they think about, plan, and manage finances and acknowledge that much of it actually *is* within their control. They can decide that hope is not a viable plan. It requires hard work and constant attention. They must be honest with themselves, even if it means making difficult, unpopular decisions. It is about taking responsibility and paying attention.

ENSURE THAT EVERYONE HAS A ROLE

Finances are everyone's responsibility, from the visitors' desk to the boardroom. Everyone has a role to play, and everyone has a responsibility to be vigilant and concerned about the management and oversight of finances. If it only rests with a select few, not only will monitoring suffer, but poor decisions will result. Only a fully engaged organization will create responsible financial management.

Institutions must take the attitude that finances impact everyone and all have a role in making the balance sheet a healthy one. The staff should have reasonable access to the budget and routine financial reports to better understand institutional challenges and feel they are part of the solution. Such a shared approach results in better decisions, more thorough consideration, and investment in the success of an organization's financial health. It also lessens the chances of fraud, theft, embezzlement, and other untoward activity when *everyone* is invested and aware. And, of course, trustees must be conversant with the finances and feel comfortable with and fully understand the implications of their decisions.

It is essential that we share financial information and discuss it throughout the organization, encouraging questions and suggestions and providing a safe environment to speak out if staff perceives a contradiction or problem. Every organization should be willing to fully utilize all available staff resources to hear new perspectives, cost-cutting measures, or revenue-producing ideas—especially from those who are closest to the action on an everyday basis.

Prudent financial management is an important trustee responsibility, but as a practical matter, much of that responsibility is delegated to and owned by the entire staff, not just the department heads. And for the staff to own and understand the implications and challenges of museum finance, information must be shared with them. Having a shared understanding of challenges makes it easier for the entire organization to be budget conscious and understand and support institutional decisions and why they are made.

Everyone has a role. When more people are involved, surprises are minimized, good ideas have a voice, and the entire museum has been awakened to financial realities.

Remember that above all, museum finance is about balancing money and mission, paying attention and making difficult decisions. And remember—hope alone is not enough!

NOTES

1. "Art Museums by the Numbers 2015," Association of Art Museum Directors, January 7, 2016, https://aamd.org/our-members/from-the-field/art-museums-by-the-numbers-2015.
2. Ford W. Bell, "How Are Museums Supported Financially in the U.S.?" United States Department of State, https://static.america.gov/uploads/sites/8/2016/03/You-Asked-Series_How-Are-Museums-Supported-Financially-in-the-US_English_Lo-Res_508.pdf.

Index

trust: confidentiality and, 98–99; ethics and, 12, 13, 14, 30, 95–96; with oversight, 112–22; public, 1, 7, 12, 92, 95, 99, 115

trustees, role of, 84–89, 93–94, 100–101, 109, 111–13, 119, 121, 134. *See also* business, museum; volunteers

Tupper Lake Heritage Museum, New York, 15

Type Museum, London, 21

uncertainty, two types of, 58

the unexpected: expansion with, 77–78; museum business with, 83

United Arab Emirates, 73

university museums, 14

University of Georgia, 16

University of Missouri-Kansas City, 35

U.S. Treasury Bonds, 59

Utah, 75

value, entrepreneurship and creating, 43

Van Gogh Museum, Amsterdam, 33

Venice, Italy, 73

Vermont, 13–14, 91

Vesco, Robert, 103

veterans, World War I, 32

violations: ethics, 12, 13, 14, 95; trust, 98

Virginia, 17, 19, 38, 63, 77

Virginia Historical Society (Virginia Museum of History and Culture), 17

Virginia Museum of Fine Arts, 38, 63

Virginia Museum of History and Culture (Virginia Historical Society), 17

Virtual Drop-In Experiences, Contemporary Arts Museum Houston, 37

visitors: lack of, 16, 18; race and, 40; sophistication, 3, 14

VMFA on the Road, Virginia Museum of Fine Arts, 38

volunteers: as integral, 8, 15; trustees, 84–89, 93–94, 100–101, 109, 111–13, 119, 121, 134

Waddell & Reed, 32

Walker Art Museum, Minnesota, 34

Washington, DC, 11, 38, 54, 76

Washington, George, 38

Washington State, 17, 37, 119

Waterman, Robert H., Jr., 43, 68

Weathering the Storm campaign, 36

Werner, Paul, 64

Weserburg Mussseum of Modern Art, Germany, 33

Westchester Children's Museum, 63

West Palm Beach, Florida, 76

West Texas A&M University, 17

"What Makes Entrepreneurs Entrepreneurial?" (Sarasvathy), 41

whistleblowers, 93, 94–95, 120

Whitney Museum of American Art, New York, 31

Who Moved My Cheese? (Johnson), 66

"Winterlight Festival," Newfields, 40

Wisconsin, 31

Witte Museum, Texas, 38

Woodmere Art Museum, 17

World Video Game Hall of Fame, Strong National Museum of Play, 69

World War I, 32, 35, 41

Xerox, 42

Young, Lew, 43

About the Author

Brian Alexander has worked in museums for over forty years. He has been the president and CEO of the National World War I Museum, president and CEO of the Historic Annapolis Foundation, executive vice president and director of the Shelburne Museum, and director of the museum program for the State Historical Society of North Dakota. He has also held museum positions for the State of Illinois and County of Fairfax, Virginia. He has been an AAM accreditation reviewer and MAP consultant, member of the National Council of AASLH, grants reviewer for IMLS and NEH, and speaker/consultant on various museum administration topics. Currently he is visiting professor of museum administration at the Cooperstown Graduate Program of the State University of New York.